D0856417

GARDENING
ROUND THE YEAR

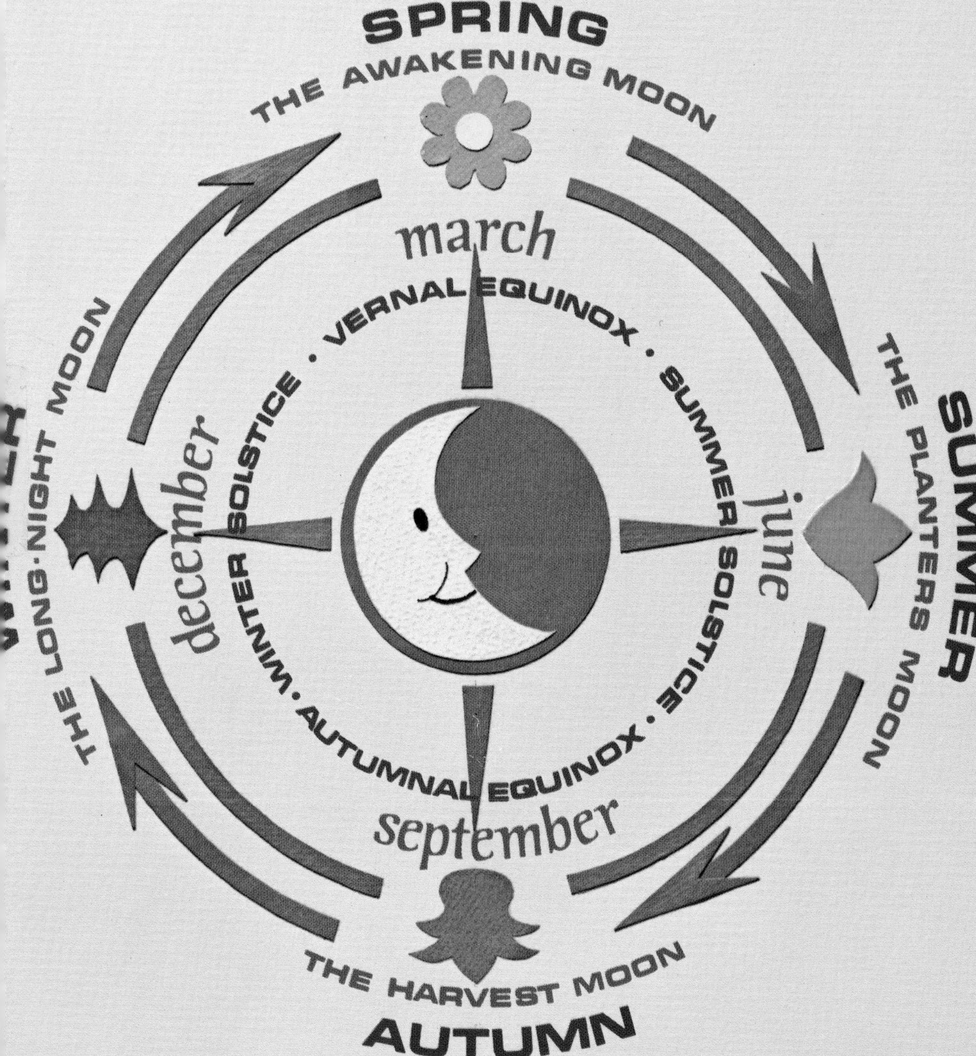

SPRING
THE AWAKENING MOON

march

VERNAL EQUINOX · SUMMER SOLSTICE

· WINTER SOLSTICE · VERNAL EQUINOX ·

SUMMER
THE PLANTERS MOON

june

THE LONG·NIGHT MOON

december

· AUTUMNAL EQUINOX · SUMMER SOLSTICE ·

september

THE HARVEST MOON
AUTUMN

margaret tipton wheatly

WITHDRAWN-UNL

Gardening
Round the Year

SAINT FIACRE
Noted herbalist, patron
saint of gardeners

Gardening Round the Year

By Margaret Tipton Wheatly
Horticultural Consultant and Columnist

Published by
Woodbridge Press Publishing Company
Santa Barbara, California 93111

Published by

Woodbridge Press Publishing Company
Post Office Box 6189
Santa Barbara, California 93111

Copyright © 1977 by Margaret Tipton Wheatly

All rights reserved.

World rights reserved. This book or any part thereof may not be reproduced in any form whatsoever without the prior written permission of Woodbridge Press Publishing Company, except in the case of brief passages embodied in critical reviews or articles.

Library of Congress Cataloging in Publication Data
Wheatly, Margaret Tipton.
  Gardening round the year.

  Includes index.
  1. Gardening. I. Title.
SB453.W425   635'.0973   77–72680
ISBN 0–912800–36–4

Published simultaneously in the United States and Canada

Printed in the United States of America

Cover design by the author; cover art by Cassie Bill and Trudi Mazzetti; drawings by Cassie Bill.
Photo credits: Page 56, Ray Borges; 88, Steve Malone—Santa Barbara News-Press; 93, Burpee Seed Co.; 118, Mendocino Botanical Garden; 54, 151, 162, Wilkins Wheatly.

Contents

Preface

The Art and Rhythm of Gardening

Gardening Round the Year is as basic and instructive as the author's previous book, *The Joy of a Home Fruit Garden*. This new work by Margaret Tipton Wheatly provides a clear and simplified method for beginning gardeners, as well as those more experienced, to get at the fundamentals and rhythms of the garden year. "The Orbit," shown on page 8, pictures graphically the lengthening and shortening days by means of the solstices and equinoxes.

Organized with care and written with warmth, inspiration and a perennial love of growing things, the book divides the monthly programs from the fundamentals of doing the actual work of making a garden.

Part I is divided into the four seasons which fill the measure of the year, beginning with spring, when the garden year commences, progressing through the excitement and rewards of planting and growing, and ending with autumn, when in most areas plants mature and harvest is the dominant activity.

Part II sets forth the fundamentals of soils, planting techniques, and plant care and management through the garden year. For those who believe they must put aside the thrills and rewards of growing things until "spring unlocks the flowers to paint the laughing soil," there is a special section devoted to growing vegetables indoors, not only for persons who live in short growing regions, but also for those who may not have land for an outside garden. This includes a discussion of miniature food plants and herbs which can be grown year-round by means of inexpensive gro-lamps and greenhouse windows for places about the house where there may be insufficient light for rapid growth.

—*The Publisher*

The Orbit

The Orbit of the Garden Year

The design on the opposite page pictures graphically the seasons through the year, and shows how the days lengthen and how they grow shorter to make for us the growing year. The moon is the earth's only satellite and makes one complete orbit of the globe each month. It also accompanies the earth in its orbit round the sun to bring about the changing seasons. (In the southern hemisphere, the orbit need only be reversed.)

At the equinoxes, day and night are of equal length. The solstices mark the longest and shortest days of the year. The months in which each celestial event occurs determine the gardener's planting times, the kind of crops to grow and the temper of the seasons that lie ahead.

For instance, the vernal (spring) equinox, coming as it does on about March 20 or 21, sets the day of spring's arrival and returning favorable planting temperatures. Days continue to lengthen until the summer solstice June 22, the longest day of the year. Then they begin to shorten very slowly, until the autumnal equinox September 23 brings day and night again to equal length. Then the days begin to grow more noticeably shorter and nights cooler. This weather pattern continues until December 22 heralds the winter solstice and we experience the shortest day of the year.

But it is good news for gardeners because with this event, days begin to lengthen and the orbit of the garden year begins once again.

Appreciation

It is difficult to thank all the persons who may have been helpful along the way toward the completion of this handbook, but special recognition is due Rachel Snyder, editor-in-chief of *Flower and Garden,* for encouragement through the years and to Jack Tillotson II, publisher of the magazine, for permission to use excerpts from my columns.

I am grateful to the many enthusiastic persons from adult garden classes who first suggested a book on this different approach to gardening 'round the year. "Just put our lessons into a book, so we can have them for reference when we are no longer in school," they said. Working with eager groups who have interesting questions makes teaching thrilling; teaching through writing for a larger audience becomes quite another experience. But as I got into it, I recalled happy classroom hours with the warm response of interested people, each vying for attention from "Teach." I hope, dear gardener, as you use this manual you get the help from it that my many students have from similar lessons in the classroom. And to those familiar friends of live garden classes, I hope you find some of the laughter we've shared together folded into the many incidents you've helped me illustrate here by your eagerness for help.

Margaret Tipton Wheatly
Santa Barbara, California

In Partnership
With Nature

To make and tend a garden is to be in partnership with nature. If we garden for where we live, we will learn what our opportunities are and make the most of them. The "orbit" on the preceding pages delineates the four seasons of the garden year—spring, summer, autumn and winter—and, because spring does not come everywhere at once, the orbit helps you to make allowances for your own particular garden. The topography of the land, altitude, latitude and longitude are factors that alter temperature and affect climate.

Take advantage of the information available near you by calling your local weather station to find your first safe planting dates in spring and the last safe growing temperatures in autumn before harvest of tender plants must be completed. The days between those events encompass your favorable growing season.

The weather pattern in the daily newspaper or on television is also a good general guide. A minimum/maximum temperature record kept faithfully day by day is also a valuable guide through the coming years, although seasons differ. Plenteous winter moisture may delay spring, but will be growth insurance for bountiful harvests later in the year.

The amount of sunshine is an important element. In colder, more northerly latitudes, where spring is much delayed and autumn is not far behind, allowances will need to be made still further and great care used when choosing varieties of plants, but once summer is with us we all experience the same glorious, abundantly bountiful nature.

After determining the date of spring's arrival and finding

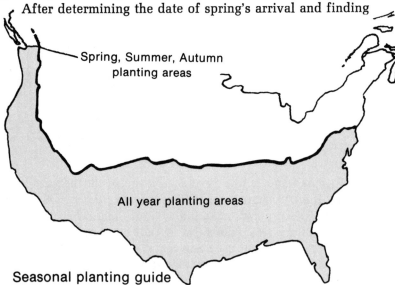

Spring, Summer, Autumn
planting areas

All year planting areas

Seasonal planting guide

To the north of the division line hardy plants survive; all-year planting areas enjoy more varieties of plant life, and subtropical zones are found in relatively limited areas; but the land mass, in general, has more moderate temperatures.

The median line of hardiness indicates the predominating temperatures and is drawn roughly between zones 5 and 6 on the USDA plant hardiness zone map.

Areas to the north of the line have fewer days of high temperatures while those to the south and west will enjoy a more favorable plant climate. Elevation is a prime factor affecting temperatures, and thermal belts are frequently found within *hardy* plant climate zones.

out the length of your growing season, you can gauge your plantings by the time suggested by the seedsman for different plants to mature. In short growing areas and those with cool summers one should take advantage of the quick-to-mature Midget Vegetable varieties which are as delicious as those that take a third more time to become table ready. More details of this easy-to-grow vegetable group will be found in chapter 6.

Late winter, with but minor adjustments, is about the same everywhere. It is the big bareroot planting season; the time of pruning, spraying and either planting or getting ready to plant deciduous ornamental plants, roses and fruits.

Even though the temperatures of spring arrive at different times across the country, we may steal a march on this momentous event by starting tender flower and vegetable plants indoors, either with the aid of a modern lighted device or the old-fashioned use of a sunny window with newspaper insulation against frost. Once you get the young plants well on their way in the shelter of the house, you may enjoy their exuberant growth pending the warming of the earth. A "greenhouse window" will provide abundant shelf space for pots and boxes of thrifty plants. (Ways to grow vegetables and herbs indoors in the most northerly latitudes are described fully in chapter 6.)

It becomes, then, the *time* we alter in doing the work, not the work itself. Once we realize this fact, a whole bright new concept of gardening opens for us. Growing plants calls for the same skills everywhere. Seasons may change considerably, as they do from North Dakota to Southern California, for example, but even gardeners living in southern lands must confine their winter garden to hardy plants.

A follow-through of work is the pattern of the garden year. One season does not leave off sharply when the next begins, as the orbit clearly shows, but blends into the one that follows. We are a few weeks into the new season before we realize it. This may be largely responsible for the anticipation gardening brings.

Part I

Gardening in Rhythm
with the Seasons

The author welcomes spring with the first strawberries.
Directions for duplicating this productive focal point for your
garden are given in Chapter 6.

Chapter 1
Spring

"When spring unlocks the flowers
to paint the laughing soil . . ."

Reginald Heber

March

Spring sets forth the garden year. Seeds stir in warming soil, days begin to lengthen and we may say "Farewell winter, welcome spring." The March moon may wear a veil of misty rain, but with the vernal equinox (about March 21) day and night are again of equal length, and soon noticeable changes will occur in plant growth.

The rhythm of the seasons brings lengthening days that dictate the kinds of plants we grow and the harvest we reap. Buds burst into flowers, leaves and new branches. While savoring this display of energy make plans for planting and spring flower shows.

Weather patterns

The gardener's spring does not always come with the regularity of timetables, but is an expression of the weather pattern that has come before. An excessively wet winter generally brings a late spring with lush growth in both animal and vegetable kingdoms. Weeds will overrun the garden, and snails, slugs, earwigs, sowbugs and cutworms will devour many choice plants. Diligence is the key word that will keep the garden whole and thriving.

Keep a garden record

At this beginning of a new garden year begin a personal garden record. Use a calendar with squares big enough for the entries, organize seasonal garden routines, club meetings, flower shows and other data you are apt to forget. Go through each month and mark important work like feeding, spraying, putting out bait for chewing insects, planting and harvest. Next year you won't need to try to recall the previous year's peak harvests, total yield and kinds that did well if you also make a chart that will show at a glance the performance of your plants. We use these entries: Date planted, Kind of plant, Amount of yield per pick, How used. If kept up for a year it will guide the planting another season.

Homegrown abundance

Early spring is the best time to begin a garden. Peas sown now should mature before mildew gets heavy. Edible pod kinds give colorful purple flowers and delicious pods to eat. Plant seeds of summer vegetables in a cold frame or sunny window to be ready for transplanting under Hotkaps in April or May, if you plan to grow these from seed.

Organize your own headstart program

You may get a headstart by planting seed of bush beans, cucumber and summer squash under Hotkaps. If the garden soil is moist enough when seed are sown, the Hotkaps will retain the moisture until small plants can be seen through the semitransparent waxed paper. When you begin to irrigate, do not remove the covers, but make a furrow around the outer edge, and follow all package directions. You might prefer to use gallon-size plastic bottles with bottoms cut away, which simulate English cloches and are unbreakable.

These devices will protect young plants against frost. Peppers, tomatoes and eggplants grown in glasshouses often appear in retail nurseries before open garden temperatures are high enough for continued growth, so to avoid stunting and even possible loss these protective devices are necessary.

They provide more than shelter against frost if a dual-purpose dust is sprinkled about before sealing the Hotkaps or bottles with a rim of soil. Sowbug/cutworm bait will be growth insurance for both seeds and plants.

Use calcium for plant health

Lessen the chance of blossom-end rot of tomatoes and peppers with a liberal use of calcium when preparing the soil for these popular summer vegetables. If your soil is alkaline use calcium sulfate (agricultural gypsum) instead of calcium carbonate (lime).

Vegetables add a new dimension to a picking garden. As winter plants begin to wane or mature, replant with heat-tolerant kinds. Lettuce is a good example, but switch to leaf kinds. Beans will replace peas. Because some leaf greens may be picked almost daily we actually spend as much time with vegetables as with flowers, and those that are grown primarily for cutting complement the vegetables perfectly.

Grow your own replacements

Consider the economy of growing plants from seed at home to save money and garden space, and to have the kinds you most want. While flowers and vegetables of the season are maturing, replacements should be coming to transplanting size. Seeds may be grown in pots, flats if a quantity of plants are needed, or in seed pans placed in either sun or shade to germinate. If you cannot meet seedlings' special needs, plan to buy established plants when the time is right to plant out in the open ground.

Keep new plants coming

Plant frequently to maintain production of both flowers and vegetables. When an annual is coming to bloom, replant with the same kind or a variety more suited to the advancing season. Head lettuce will give way to leafing kinds; green beans will replace peas; and squash and cucumbers will be a welcome change from winter vegetables.

Don't let crops mature

Frequent harvest will ensure continuous production. Do not let flowers set seed or vegetable crops mature. When annuals like sweet alyssum begin to seed, shear sharply, feed lightly and enjoy another fragrant display. Succulent salad greens are always expensive, but homegrown watercress may always be at hand by partially filling a box with good sandy loam and keeping it constantly wet. The cress may be planted from seed or roots procured from a natural planting along a stream.

A good location for a cress bed is under a faucet that drips, or one that is used frequently enough to keep the soil extra wet. Do not discard the bed when it goes to seed, because it will grow again next season.

Ornamental perennial vegetables

The bold structural leaves of green globe artichokes and the high color of rhubarb make them candidates for focal planting. Following harvest of the chokes, cut down the old leaves. Dress liberally with manure and a complete plant food and soon a bountiful new leaf crop will emerge. If you missed planting these perennial vegetables during the bareroot season, you may grow them from seed. Like other robust perennials, green globe artichokes, rhubarb and asparagus come readily from seed. Because of asparagus' rapid growth and large root system, it is best to prepare a seedbed in open ground if possible, where the roots may continue to grow. Areas for this most delectable vegetable may be bordering the conventional vegetable garden or between berry vines. Because berry plants' branches are wide spreading, the plants are set six feet apart, but the roots use only a fraction of the space between them. At least two asparagus roots can safely be planted between the Boysen, Young and Logan berry plants.

The technique of harvest of asparagus and rhubarb are important. Asparagus spears may be allowed to grow ten or even twelve inches tall for maximum yield and vitamins. Cut them on a slant well below the soil. Do not cut rhubarb stalks, but grasp a stalk well below the leaf and give a sharp pull to one side. Exuding juices will form a sanitary seal that prevents disease from entering the plant.

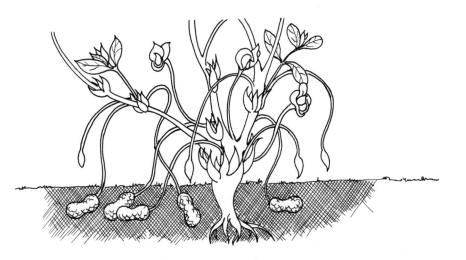

This is a peanut vine or plant. These delicious "nuts" are not true nuts. The first syllable tells us they are members of the pea family. How to begin your "peanut farm:" Plant 3 shelled nuts in "hills," spaced about 18 inches apart, in rows 3 feet apart—if more than a few hills are planted. When plants bloom, hill them up (draw the soil up about the stems). Nuts form at the tips of stems called pegs and bury themselves—thus the need for loose soil around the plant. Harvest when the plant matures and the majority of the kernels are hard. Hang the plants in a dry, airy place for several weeks. When the nuts are no longer starchy they may be cut from the plant, stored in open baskets or string bags, or shelled and roasted in the oven at 350° for about 20 minutes—or to your taste.

Beginning gardeners

We can give children a priceless heritage through gardening. Because they are generally interested in food they may find vegetable growing exciting and rewarding. Burpee seeds have developed a minigarden of easy-to-grow and quick-to-mature vegetables in seed tape that takes the guesswork out of planting. If you have or can make a very light soil bed, peanuts are an intriguing food plant which will interest parents and youngsters alike. These legumes are not only easy to grow, but fascinating in their habits. Unlike other peas or beans, "goobers" bury their seed pods that do not open when ripe. Peanuts may be dry roasted in a popcorn popper to suit the exact taste of the young gardener.

Adults too may become avid food farmers when the advantages of homegrown produce are considered. They may enjoy kinds not grown commercially, or varieties not suited to large packing operations. They may appreciate being able to harvest vine-, bush- or tree-ripened delicate-fleshed fruits and vegetables of gourmet quality.

The advancing season

Plant for the summer that lies ahead. Harvest asparagus, rhubarb, and berries, and get ready for systematic and continuous irrigation, feeding, and diligent control of insects and fungi to ensure bountiful crops, but be alert to the kinds of chemicals you use. Protect nature's own controls.

Harvest late spring peas, head lettuce and root vegetables. Onions may become thrips-infested. Replant with vegetables that not only endure heat but require it to grow quickly. If some young plants have been growing in flats you are jumps ahead; if not, buy plants from whoever grows what you need.

Green beans, summer squash, corn, cucumber, watermelon and cantaloupe are a few that provide appetizing meal makings. The so-called winter squash is misleading and confusing to beginning gardeners, because it grows during summer like other squash. "Keeping" squash would be a more understandable term.

Warmer days bring plants to maturity sooner. For soil health, rotate kinds of plants grown each season in beds where possible. If you think space for vegetables is too limited look about for unconventional ways to grow at least some salad vegetables. Small bush-type tomatoes will be conversation (and nibble) plants when grown in pots and baskets on the terrace (see section on gardening in containers in chapter 6).

Where space is limited for annuals—either flower or vegetable—compute the time from seed to harvest and plant those that take a long time to come to maturity in individual beds; otherwise, later planting will be hampered, because the soil cannot be worked for later summer planting. Here are some examples; onions and carrots, radishes and leaf lettuce are good catch (between) crops. Eggplant, corn, peppers and tomatoes bear all summer and need the warmest area in the garden.

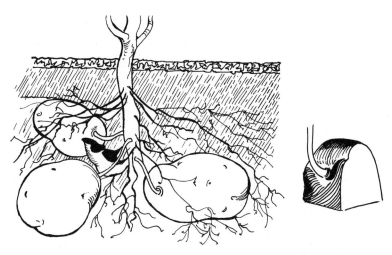

A hill of Irish potatoes. A new seed piece—that will produce the harvest. The sketch shows how the potatoes grow out from the stalk that is produced by the "eye" of the seed piece. It is important to plant in well-tilled soil, and keep well cultivated throughout the growing season.

Grow beauty

Some vegetables are showy enough to grow with flowers. In addition to green globe artichokes and rhubarb, eggplant with its two-inch nightshade purple flowers attracts much attention in our garden during summer. Rhubarb (red) chard gives continuous colorful succulent salad and/or cooking greens. Many culinary herbs are pleasing in foliage and flowers. Showy red spikes of pineapple sage flowers are a favorite with hummingbirds.

Potatoes in variety

When you hear the word *potato* do you visualize mealy Irish, red- or white-skinned, sweet or yams? These popular tubers do not all belong to the same family so their culture is entirely different. Consider the Irish kind first. Where space allows (you will need two square feet for each hill), you may harvest a good crop of *Solanum tuberosa*, provided you have loamy soil. Even more important than soil is the kind of stock you plant. Alway get certified *seed* potatoes. Domestic (eating kinds) may carry potato diseases, which infest not only potatoes but beets, turnips and carrots.

Keep the soil pH about 6.5 with soil sulfur, or you may use peat moss as a humus dressing which will conserve moisture and keep the soil acid. Avoid using lime or wood ash; however, agricultural gypsum (calcium sulfate) may be used as a dressing and in the preparation of the soil before planting.

The principal difference between sweet potatoes and yams is in texture. Sweets are generally dry-fleshed, while yams are moist and higher in color. Choose the kind your family likes best. You grow them the same way. If your introduction to sweet potatoes consists of growing one in water and enjoying the cascading vine as it wends its way over your living room, you may want to try growing a hill or two in the garden.

Unlike Irish potatoes, which are planted from a portion of the tuber, sweets are planted from slips which are often available from farm supply houses, or you may start your own. Some persons do this the same way you begin to grow one in water. When the young plants are about four inches high break them carefully from the potato, and if the soil is warm, plant them in the garden.

If you want to start the conventional way, bury a whole tuber in sand or vermiculite, and set the pot in a warm place (about 70° F.). In about a month small plants will emerge. When these are three or four inches high uncover the potato carefully and remove the sprouts with a heel (small portion of the parent tuber). Plant when the soil is warm, or grow them on in small pots.

Get expert advice

Either your county farm adviser or state department of agriculture will have comprehensive bulletins on the growing and harvesting of these delectable foods, but a few remarks will also be insurance toward success. In crop rotation, last year's corn rows or other grain soil is recommended. Aftercare is important, or you may lose the harvest.

Unlike Irish potatoes which are elegant companions to new peas when these happen to come at the same time, the sweet or yam kinds must be mature before harvesting.

Good exposure makes for easy harvest

Plant pole beans along an east- or south-facing path for ease of harvest. Most of the beans will be borne on the sunny side of the plants. Patented string trellises do away with the old-time forest of poles and tedious tying up. In addition to the two strong end stakes, a top member will be needed to support the heavy weight of the crop of beans. Plants readily wind about the lattices. This treated material should last two seasons, so if you feel thrifty, remove the vines by cutting away the heavy bearing nodes and clipping the twining stems frequently so they will unwind easily. Any nonlegume plant will be good crop rotation.

Seasonal finish line

By March's end we are nearing the end of the bareroot season. Be alert when buying bareroot plants then, because only top-quality plants will have a chance to survive. Keep watch over newly planted bareroot stock to make sure they are beginning to grow. Swelling buds are good news that roses and/or fruiting plants are alive and well.

Protect new roses that are slow leafing with a drape of burlap or other porous cloth to avoid sunburn. Whitewash deciduous tree trunks to avoid sunburn until a leaf canopy will grow to shade the stem structure.

Get the ground ready first

Following winter rains the soil may be almost as firmly packed as though it has not been worked at all. Spading the soil without adding considerable humus really does little good, because after a rain or as soon as we begin to irrigate, it settles together again. If the soil is adobe or clay, add three pounds of agricultural gypsum per square foot of soil for conditioning.

Soil renovation should continue until manure is spread on the entire garden. Because manures seldom provide the three basic elements—nitrogen, phosphoric acid and potash—in sufficient amounts for total plant nourishment, they need to be supplemented with whichever element is lacking.

The practice of using agricultural gypsum (calcium sulfate) for fly control in chicken houses takes care of phosphoric acid and the use of peat moss to absorb moisture improves chicken manure by adding humus which is generally lacking and lowers the pH as well.

The value of manure aside from its nitrogen is the physical effect the organic matter and enzymes have on the soil, as may be seen by the table in chapter 7. Manures vary in plant food value because of the way in which they are handled on the farm and the different forage fed to animals.

Maintain total nutrition throughout the garden with a complete plant food. Biweekly feeding should give maximum yield of annual flowers and vegetables (once a month for perennials), but keep watch for hunger signs, which include slowing growth, a pale, wan look and falling production.

When using organic plant foods allow a month or longer for the nutrients to become available. Anticipate plants' needs with prior applications. Inversely, inorganic plant foods give quick pickups. The two kinds may be applied at once; this is the way time-release nutrients work.

Established citrus and avocado trees will respond to a dressing of high-nitrogen fertilizer. An analysis like 20–10–10 will not only bring quick response but will also provide the other elements for abundant yield and sustained vigor. If frost may possibly come to your garden, delay this application until all danger of frost is past.

Don't get weed-happy!

Following a spring rain weed growth can be measured by a yardstick. By the time soil is dry enough for any operation but pulling, we may get weed-happy. Avoid browse-weeding —nipping a weed here and one there, like a cow turned into lush pasture. That manner of weeding accomplishes little except dirtying your hands, shoetoes and pant-knees. Weeding, like other garden chores, requires planning. Get ready to weed with proper and adequate tools: gloves, weeding boxes or baskets, canvas for larger sizes, rubber kneeling pad and boxes for uprooted seedlings for replanting. Then you are ready to tackle those omnipresent weeds. Spring weeding is a step toward efficient insect and fungi control as well as a neat tidy garden.

Bermuda and nutgrass, both dormant during cold weather, begin to green up with spring warmth. If you plan to rely entirely on manual control of these you will find much enjoyable garden time (and energy) consumed in edging beds and paths where Bermuda grass is one of the lawn plants. Nutgrass (a sedge) will appear in bulb plantings and other well-tilled and fertilized areas. It defies digging and pulling at its lush green grass-like leaves only tends to distribute it by means of the small "nuts" that break off and start new plants. Safe chemicals are available for weed control to aid in this unending battle. Ask your county farm adviser for bulletins listing these valuable garden helpers.

Home gardeners report ingenious means of applying herbicides to control individual kinds of weeds. They paint Bermuda grass along paths and garden bed edges with a smallish paint brush, or make a protective spray plant shield by removing one side and an end of a paper carton. Both methods are safe and effective for control of noxious weeds and grasses growing among desirable plants.

Make a spray or dust shield by cutting away one side of a box. This enclosure effectively prevents insecticide from drifting onto plants not intended to be treated.

Spring is a big weeding time

Use many methods and devices to suit the condition and size of weeds. A modern labor-saving way to weed beyond the cultivated places is with the power mower. Use an old blade and set the mower to its highest notch. Mow alternate weeks or when the weeds are about six inches tall.

Seasonal weeds are a price we pay to live in an all-year garden climate, but no matter where we garden spring and summer weeds will pop up to vex us and take time away from pleasanter tasks. During spring weeding various methods can be employed to rid the garden of these unwelcome intruders which rob the soil of food and moisture and act as insect and disease incubators. Consider nature's activities and pace your garden program to them. Everything doesn't have to be done in a single day. Take one chore at a time.

Unplanted plots overgrown with young weeds may be hoed over quickly. An efficient way to weed a plot with volunteer flower plants is to remove those first, then hoe over the ground and replant the flower seedlings—a double job in double time. Weeding and mulching go hand in hand. As we go through the plantings, discarding not only weeds but surplus volunteer plants, we create a dust mulch; additional material applied then will help with weed control, conserve moisture and aid plant growth (see details in chapter 7).

Lengthening days bring changes in activity when we are but a month into the spring season. March often brings the first burst of summer temperatures and the last chance for spring showers. Moisture falling on warming earth may bring unnoticed weeds to seed in a twinkling. The cheese weed (a mallow) is host to rust spores, measuring worms and aphids—truly one of the worst garden weeds. Waste no time getting it out of the garden.

Now is an auspicious time to keep the promises of last year when dandelions overran the lawn. These deep-rooted plants blooming gaily over the turf may look like a mountain meadow, but as summer comes on you will have an untidy greensward decorated with numerous seed stalks. Modern chemicals take much of the backache out of weeding. I like to use a complete treatment and relax in the knowledge that the lawn is weeded, fed and guarded against fungi attacks. For a true naturalist and Sunday afternoon conversation, a fun way to weed out dandelions is to let a land turtle do the job. But if you are bent on making delicious wine, let the dandelions grow for the enjoyment of the beverage.

Stop, look and listen

Tune in on garden wildlife by listening for different sounds and rhythms. "Stop, look and listen" is a good motto to apply to pest control. Stop long enough to make sure your identification is correct. Look to find out the extent of the infestation and listen for the sound of chewing insects. A wasp working on dry plant stems, preparing a nest, makes a rasping noise, while insects chewing on green leaves produce a soft muffled sound.

Consider the useful creatures that inhabit the garden and learn which are friend or foe before swatting, spraying, dusting or squashing under a firm boot. Toads and lizards are garden benefactors which we sometimes squeal at the sight of. Gopher and king snakes are often wrongly killed, yet these desirable creatures work on the extermination squad every day of the week.

Lizards are among the beneficial creatures that inhabit almost every garden. Their choice viands are measuring worms, sow and pill bugs and other small wildlife that happens along their way.

Another defender we may fail to recognize is the ladybird beetle. Even if we can identify them from various other navy bean-size beetles, we may not distinguish their *A*-shaped ravenous larvae (which destroy more aphids than a bottle of spray or can of dust) and pinch them to death, if that is your preferred method of eliminating crawling things.

Declare war on garden enemies by eliminating hiding places under boards and debris for snails, slugs and earwigs. Weeding boxes left for a day or so on the ground are favorite areas. Elevate plant tubs on bricks or stones or make complete contact with the earth. With a long-handled spoon place bait well beneath the planters, out of the way of pets and leaching effect of moisture.

Burlap pupating bands provide complete winter protection for the ladybird beetle's pupae which will emerge in the spring as active adults. Make the bands from strips of burlap long enough to go around tree trunks, or other sheltered areas, and pin in place with a nail. The cloth should be at least four inches wide after being folded a few times.

Efficient distribution system

Effective pest control begins with efficient equipment. Water-impelled spray devices that screw on a garden hose are as easy to use as conventional nozzles and other sprinkling devices.

In addition to the well-known protective poison sign on garden insecticides, become aware of a comparable warning that cautions us in the use of sprays on sensitive plants. For your plant's protection always read the directions on the package. In the ·meantime, it may help to know a few everyday groups of plants that may be injured: most ferns, camellias and garden violets.

Pump-dispenser hand lotion bottles make ideal containers for liquid plant food and/or spray chemicals. The pump even measures the fluid for mixing with water once its output is determined, and does away with spilled plant food and bottle caps that refuse to unscrew after a few times of using. Another way to get ahead of rusting bottle caps is to replace them with tight-fitting corks.

One step forward

As the season advances we catch a breath, straighten our backs and take a long look about us to evaluate the effect of all the trimming, clipping and grooming with shears, sprays, food and water. Pause to admire the daily development of exciting blooms, ripening fruits and maturing vegetables. When we garden joyfully our entire lookout changes. No longer is digging a spot for flowers or vegetables back-breaking toil, because our focus is far ahead on the results.

If an incentive is needed when preparing garden soil, spade as if you were digging fishing worms—a formula for the serious gardener with fun on his mind.

What does one get out of gardening besides improving the neighborhood? Uplift of spirit! Herein lies the great value of a daily tour of the garden. "But," someone says, "what possible changes can come in one day?" That all depends upon one's outlook. Because plants are not static, and continuous growth comes to each individual plant, there must be discernible changes. Learn to anticipate maturity of flower, fruit, vegetable or seed every day; these are some of the little things to look for.

It is the growth factor that gives gardening much of its appeal. Subtle changes characterize plants. How many of these surprises one is able to discover and enjoy enables a joyful gardener to rate his day.

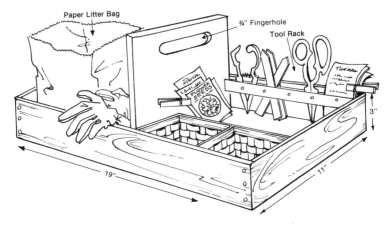

Easy-to-make "tool-tray" or harvest box.

April

April brings advancing spring. With nature it doesn't matter whether it is a weed, a prize wildflower, a mosquito larva or the rarest butterfly—when the time is right, new life comes forth.

Between the growth of catkins and leaves nature seems to delay her burst of energy as if to give gardeners a moment to reflect and to enjoy the flourishing earth. Perhaps nothing says *spring* like fruit blossoms. Cut long sprays of flowering fruit boughs for bouquets and prune at the same time.

"All danger of frost is past" is a most welcome announcement by the fruit-frost service or weather forecaster for regions that may expect killing frost as late as the end of March or mid-April. However, if your garden is on one of the cold islands in the midst of subtropical splendor or a cold region, don't cast off the coverings of plants and otherwise disregard catering to winter. We learn patience as gardeners along with whatever else of wisdom we may gain.

Frost-damaged plants that have not begun to grow by mid-April are probably dead. Learn which plants are tender to frost, other extremes of climate and salt-laden air, and replace those with plants known to be hardy. Discover how to harden plants for winter before another cold season comes (see chapter 6).

Well-ordered routine

April is the beginning of true spring weather and seasonal feeding, spraying for aphids and mildew control, and harvest of flowers and vegetables. A systematic routine for chores that are repeated again and again in all seasons like a pleasant refrain doesn't mean getting in a rut, but helps avoid too-long gaps in important routines and will spell success.

Consider how seasonal chores follow each other to make for well-ordered rhythm. For instance, don't water until weeding is done, and feed at the end of watering. Sow dry and set wet has long been garden lore but it can't be taken literally, because soil moisture is required to germinate seed. It means not to water immediately before planting and to run water in furrows and/or hills shortly before setting young plants from boxes or pots.

Planting techniques

When planting draw the moist soil from the sides of furrows or holes around young plants and firm in gently. After a few days plants may need moisture. Seeds should not be watered before young plants appear, except in very dry weather. Covering seed beds with burlap or other airy cloth will aid in keeping the soil moist.

During any big transplanting season we need to mark small seedlings. Colored toothpicks work well, and not only show where young plants are set, but allow you to use the same color scheme if replanting is needed. Inexpensive golf tees are more permanent.

Gardeners need to have both hindsight and foresight. If you plan to grow some plants from seed sow them well in advance of transplanting time. A way I find successful is to make seed rows in open soil, between plants that will give some shelter—the vegetable garden provides ideal conditions. If sown thinly, seedlings can remain until transplanting size and save tedious pricking off. Warning: don't let the young plants get too large before moving them to wider growth areas.

Small-structured plants like lobelia, which are good late winter into spring bloomers, and chives, which are delectable in many foods, should be planted in "hills" and transplanted in those small clumps rather than singly.

Spring work begins at different times, and depends upon the temperature, not only of a particular region, but the exposure of various beds—those in shade, being cooler than open sunlit places, will be slower to come alive. Here are some typical chores: dig and divide last year's clumps of chrysanthemum, perennial asters and other herbaceous plants. Discard old woody stems and use only vigorous outer shoots. Reset in soil newly nourished with manure, and dress with low-nitrogen plant food.

Plan for color

When we think of the spring garden we may visualize "hosts of golden daffodils." This spring glory can be repeated for several weeks with summer-flowering bulbs, tubers and roots to make the garden more exciting and perhaps even a challenge. Pink amaryllis, agapanthus and dwarf cannas are worth a try. Unless you have kept up with improved forms of cannas there's excitement aplenty—in both color and stature hybridists have worked magic.

Alstroemaria (Peruvian lily) bears long stems of exquisite orchid-like flowers for bouquets or garden color. They should not be lifted and divided needlessly, but on occasion you may want to extend the planting or to share with a friend. This is a favorable time. Dress all bulb beds with super-phosphate and use a low-nitrogen food to sustain growth of summer-flowering plants.

Place dahlia tubers in sand, or other rooting medium like vermiculite, if you wish to propagate by greenwood slips as many dahlia experts do, rather than by planting the tubers. When the shoots are about three inches high carefully remove them from the old tuber, set them in half shade in the same rooting medium blended with half sand until roots develop, then pot them as you might any young plant, and grow on until they reach garden size. By this method an expensive tuber may produce a half-dozen plants.

To prepare planting areas for dahlia tubers, make either a trench twelve inches deep and twelve inches wide, or individual holes. An advantage of the trench is that quick-to-flower seedling dahlias may be interplanted. Do this only if you grow the big kinds for fun, not to win the coveted trophy at the autumn show.

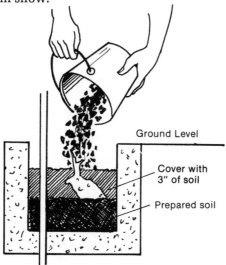

A well-planted dahlia tuber is assurance of better quality summer-into-autumn flowers. More directions on growing this popular bloomer are given in this chapter.

Ground covers

Ground-cover plants provide carpets for bare earth, face down taller plants to path edge, mask maturing bulb foliage and give diminutive blooms for miniature bouquets. Chosen with care, they will give color throughout the year with flowers and tapestry-like foliage. Shrubby rather than carpeting kinds are best where tree droppings may lodge on them.

Shearing time comes to the garden following exuberant spring bloom. Most small perennials, annuals and chamomile ground cover will be more presentable if spring flowers are shorn off. Don't leave stem ends; clip right down to the foliage for neatness. Hedge shears are just right for this performance. Chamomile is as carefree a greensward as any plant. It is not a complete substitute for grass because it is tender to foot traffic. Lay a stepping stone path across it to lead to other areas of the garden. If planted in filtered shade or an east exposure, it will fill its niche with distinction. Flowers left to mature will develop a hummocky growth.

Exciting new plants

When only a few plants of a kind are needed it is often wise to buy them and use the time of tedious seedling care for more important garden management and/or enjoyment of your own little world.

This is a good month to search nurseries for something new to brighten the garden. Because it may be repotting time some bargains may be found if one is diligent. My experience proves that herbaceous perennials are "best buys," because they generally respond to division and food. Woody plants may prove disappointing if a serious rootbound condition has developed, since it is difficult to overcome.

Spring pruning

There is scarcely a month in the year when some pruning is not in order. Shape cotoneaster, pyracantha and other berried shrubs while in bloom for more even berry distribution. Avoid legginess of *Jasmine primulinum*, quince, forsythia and other shrubs that grow long "whip" boughs by pruning either while in bloom or as they complete flowering.

Begin training new shrub and tree branches before they become too stiff to bend. Use twisted withes or twigs the length required to space the boughs—usually about twelve inches long, of about pencil size. After being twisted together the free ends are placed over the branches being separated.

Spring pruning is an important phase of garden maintenance. Between pinching back stems of annuals to removing major branches of trees lies the everyday directing of wayward branches throughout the garden. Boughs of flowering shrubs and vines need shortening following bloom to encourage new growth for next year's color parade. Prune for production and to control plant size. Considered separately and in sequence they are not so overwhelming, because one follows the other as night the day.

With the aid of twisted, flexible twigs, begin training new tree or shrub branches before they become too stiff to bend. Choose lengths required to space the boughs, usually about 12 inches—and pencil size. After being twisted together, the free ends are placed over the branches to be separated. This clever device requires no tying, does not chafe, but gives gentle guidance.

There are two phases of pruning: refurbishing and maintenance of productive wood. Observe spring-flowering plants while in bloom to see which branches are giving color. Remove heavy wood that is showing little growth and not only improve that plant's appearance but open the plant to light, which induces new growth this season. Here is a good rule to follow: cut out or shorten back a third of the flowering branches each spring after or during bloom if quantities of branches are wanted for bouquets. Strictly flowering fruits (as opposed to fruiting kinds) should be pruned severely— peaches to within six to eight inches of old wood— which forces out an abundance of long boughs that develop flower buds for next spring's display. The same technique will pay off with flowering plants that bloom at other seasons.

To keep new trees in balance pinch the ends of branches (terminal buds) from the stronger, more vigorous growing limbs to avoid too much growth to the detriment of other branches. With spring growth tree canopies may become too heavy for the trunk. Correct this condition by removing some limbs entirely. Simply to cut a branch halfway will multiply the condition you hope to correct, by inducing a proliferation of dormant buds nearer the trunk of the tree.

Thin your fruit

June fruit drop, which is recommended in colder regions, is an outmoded idea for warm latitudes and is far too late for early-ripening peaches, plums and apricots which may already have been harvested. Spring thinning will eliminate the overburden of fruit set and give gourmet quality.

A good rule of thumb is to leave space between each fruit equal to the mature fruit—one and one-half inches for apricots and plums, two to four inches for peaches. When removing the fruit, give a slight twist, rather than a straight pull. Remove those from the top of limbs. Fruit on the underside is protected from sunburn and the ever-watchful eyes of fruit-eating birds—linnets, sparrows and the lyrical mocking birds.

Leaving fruit on the tree for gradual use can be a common cause of declining citrus harvest. Mature fruit uses food which should be channeled to growing new fruit wood. Another facet of this prolonged harvest, particularly in tangerine varieties, is a pithiness which develops as the sugar and juices of the fruit are reabsorbed by the tree. So the adage "harvest in due season" takes on new and deeper meaning.

To increase fruit yield from trees that require cross-pollination you may graft in the needed varieties now or wait until June to make live bud introductions. Why not try both? Another aspect of growing more than one variety of fruit on a tree is to cut down on the amount of fruit of one kind. For instance, an entire tree of one kind of peach or apricot may be just too much. But if more than one kind is grown on one tree, harvest is extended over a longer period.

Consider plant thirst

In a land of brief winter and scarce moisture pay special attention to the water needs of plants—those that lose their leaves, as well as evergreens, and especially those newly set out. One drying out may mean failure to grow. If winter rains or snows have been light, water the entire garden thoroughly before the luxuriant spring growth begins to wane. Depending upon the lateness of rains, April may be the beginning of season-long watering. Look for these moisture shortage signs: limpness of new growth, failure of plants to mature, drooping flower stalks.

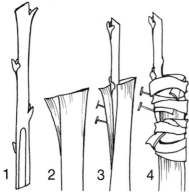

Grafting procedures

1. 3-inch scion, or bud stick, with slant-cut which will be placed against the cambium cell wall.

2. Branch to receive the scion is cut off and a slit to receive the new plant variety is made in the bark. Carefully open the bark to permit the wedge of the scion to be pushed under the bark.

3. New scion in place, and secured with two small nails (brads).

4. New scion securely fastened by ⅜ inch rubber strips (nails will be absorbed by plant sap). This phase of "top working" fruit trees is done just as buds begin to swell (flow of sap) in early spring while the scion is still dormant.

A paper sack with windows cut out for ventilation will provide shelter from the elements while the new fruit variety is beginning to grow.

Budding diagrams

1. ¾ inch by ⅜ inch bud scale, to carry the new plant variety.

2. The parent plant (tree or rose) with *window* to receive the bud scale, removed. Try to have them the same size.

3. Bud scale in place.

4. Bud scale secured firmly against the moist cambium cell wall with ⅜ inch rubber. Make the binding quite tight. Budded branch will be shortened to force the tree sap into the new bud. This phase of "top working" trees or budding roses is begun as the tree begins summer growth and the sap is flowing freely.

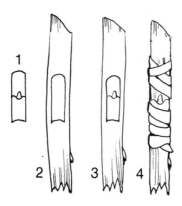

Get to know your watering devices

During the long months of watering, gather enough hoses and different kinds of sprinklers to take care of at least one area at a time, which means less labor in moving devices. An oscillating type sprinkler with various settings is quite versatile, but any new gadget calls for experimentation to learn its full potential as a useful tool. Various watering devices are needed to meet the needs of individual plants. Sprinklers that put out a soft spray, versatile seeper hoses for long strips of lawn or borders and deep soaking, or shrub sprinkler heads on portable standards are some proven types that double for permanent underground water systems. Half-round openings are ideal for use along paths, while quarter-round openings are best for corners (see chapter 7).

Set up a water program as late spring comes. Determine how much moisture various plants in your garden will need. For example: annuals, both flower and vegetable, will grow with six inches of soil moisture. Trees, shrubs and perennials may require from two to four feet.

Because winter rains or snows are frequently light and summer rains may be entirely lacking, it is often necessary to begin watering plants in early spring and to continue until autumn rains return. To lessen this burden, both for yourself and the water supply, it is wise to landscape much of the garden with drought-enduring plants that will survive long rainless summers with minimum water. Use the water ration for fruits, vegetables and choice plants nearer the house and in the patio.

Sprinkling simulates rain

I favor sprinkling over other methods of water application because of the added bonus we get: birds drinking and bathing in softly falling water. Later in summer the coolness and humidity sprinkling creates is most refreshing. The use of water as a life-sustaining force for plants should not preclude consideration and appreciation of water as an element of garden design. Here is shown an attractive bamboo water spout which is easy to construct.

Bamboo Water Spout

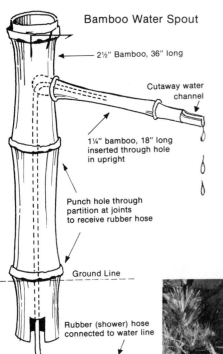

← 2½" Bamboo, 36" long

Cutaway water channel

1¼" bamboo, 18" long inserted through hole in upright

Punch hole through partition at joints to receive rubber hose

Ground Line

Rubber (shower) hose connected to water line

Enjoy the cooling, musical sound of water dripping into a waterstone or basin with an interesting and easy-to-make bamboo water spout. Follow the diagram shown here for exact details.

A water stone is an interesting detail in this oriental design garden where the bamboo water spout keeps the surrounding festuca grass and moss moist, from an hour or two of running—or a mere drip can be allowed to perform the task with less tending.

Even the drip of a leaky faucet will keep a water stone filled, providing reflections and constant hospitality for birds. The scant overflow will be enough moisture for a planting of small native ferns and a natural habitat for friendly garden frogs and toads whose voices lend enchantment to summer nights. In repayment for this hospitality they will help rid the garden of sowbugs and other chewing creatures.

Garden toads and frogs are among our best friends. A curiously hinged tongue enables toads to catch insects on the wing.

Mischievous spring rains

Just when we think the rains are over for the season and leave garden tools under a tree or a wheelbarrow of manure uncovered, we are awakened by the sound of soft rain. Spring sprinkles–not wet enough, generally, to call rain—upset well-laid plans to keep the garden chores under control. This moistening means that odd corners which we've weeded and "laid-by," so to speak, for the summer will in a trice be overgrown with weeds from seeds we've planted with diligent hoeing of the ground. This makes work we had not counted on, but weeding is just as necessary as any other garden chore, unpleasant as we may think it. Nevertheless a generous spring rain would be the garden's best Easter gift. It was a genuine optimist who penned "April showers bring May flowers." He failed to give us the name of the plant that could work such magic, but I suspect it was a weed.

Jobs put aside for a rainy day are important to our garden psyche, because to be doing something to bring the delights of spring nearer fruition is like seeing the first butterfly or bluebird of the season. When it is too wet even to set foot on the soil we may putter at tool renovation, cleaning and preparing pots and planters, making stakes for the new garden season and sowing seed flats. A great boon to gardeners who do not store some potting soil out of the rain are the packaged soil mixes. In a light rainfall area we tend to put off preparation for a few rainy days, but if such work is done beforehand a rainy day in the garden shed, or best of all a small greenhouse, can be replete with deep satisfaction.

Age new flower pots by soaking or wetting occasionally before planting, and clean old ones. Never plant in dirty pots. Washing pots and seed flats is the most lowly of garden chores, but also a very necessary one. To avoid a buildup of this work clean them as they are unplanted, when the soil is still soft. I use a swab of dry burlap to loosen all the most stubborn dirt; a good stiff brush also works magic. Greenhouse pots should be sterilized before reuse. Copper sulfate or Clorox in solution are effective.

All work and no play makes even ardent gardeners weary. Visit farming areas to get the feel and spirit of spring, which may be all about us. Sniff the peculiar scent of newly turned earth; lift your head to take in the aroma of freshly cut grass; and see hills painted white or pink with almond or peach bloom; and you will know spring is here!

May

Gemini is the zodiac sign for May, and that is fitting because with the rush of work we may wish we were twins. Here are some things to do: change the form of plants through light but frequent pruning, improve soil texture with humus, push plants toward maturity with light applications of plant food, and take time to sit in a favorite spot and enjoy the glories of your own small created world.

Poets of old sang praises to the merry month of May. After a long and dreary winter had passed, they could get on with spring garden chores. How merry the month of May is in your garden depends upon the routine you maintain. Gardening is enjoyable only when we are able to keep a little ahead of seasonal chores—planting and tending, spraying, pruning, watering and harvest.

Many gardens are brimming over with color this month. Annuals are prima donnas in almost any season. Although the ubiquitous sweet alyssum will soon seed unless the old flower heads are kept shorn, they fill gaps between developing perennials at the path edge. Candytuft will do the same for

44

the middle distance, while snapdragons and larkspur will provide background color. If space permits, gay biennials like foxglove and canterbury bells will give profuse color in early summer, but why wait two seasons for bloom when herbaceous perennials will flower each season and increase in beauty each year?

A really splendid hardy herbaceous perennial, *anemone japonica* (windflower) will display a canopy of shimmering white flowers through August and into September. Increases by the spreading roots.

We can almost mark the passing of the seasons by the plants that are in the nurseries. Exciting ones now are summer-flowering bulbs that give great promise of beauty. Some that do well in pots will concentrate color where it is wanted. These include pink and yellow calla roots, and *Tigridia* (often called the Mexican daylily, which is misleading because it is not a *Hemerocallis*, although it is true the exquisite blooms last but a day).

Try to get plants that have been accumulating in pots or cans and that are not intended for tub culture into the ground to lessen time-consuming hand watering. This is particularly important when anticipating a summer vacation.

Plant some versatile hanging plants

This spring begin the container garden with forethought, imagination and in earnest. Avoid placing baskets and pots at head-banging height; place them either at or below eye level—not only for safety but for greater enjoyment of form and color. We can emulate Cordoba, Spain, by creating a festival of color on garden and/or house walls with various kinds of potted plants. Use hanging baskets and pots from brackets and/or permanent hooks screwed into either wood or masonry walls or supported by clever devices along wall tops like that shown here.

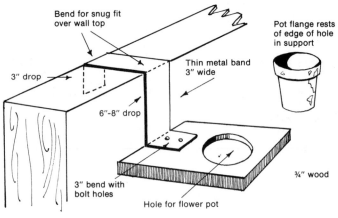

For a festival of color on house or garden walls hang baskets and/or pots from hooks screwed into either wood or masonry walls, or by clever devices along walls tops like the one shown here.

So plan now for flowering summer hanging plants that will trail splendor about your garden. Upright-growing and side-sprouting forms will also add charm and fragrance to the terrace where pleasant summer hours may be whiled away.

As the time approaches to pot up begonias, gloxinias and caladium roots it is important to have the correct soil mix. For superior quality plants and flowers the soil in which tuberous begonias grow should be renewed each season. It is not good practice to go out into the garden and scoop up soil to fill a pot because garden soil seldom contains elements in the right proportion to sustain growth, to absorb and retain moisture and to have the correct pH rating that soils of high humus content generally contain.

Soil scientists favor a nearly sterile element whose nutritive value can be controlled over planter mixes with nutrients. Most plants grown in containers do best in a fibrous soil that holds moisture well and is slightly on the acid side. After a month or so of growth most plants may need a bit more food, and some adjustment may be advisable in the plant food formula depending upon the plants' needs and luxuriance of foliage. An advantage of using peat moss as a volume material is its light weight and copious water-holding capacity—a point worth considering where several hanging plants are grown.

If you are in a hanging-basket rut with tuberous begonias and fuchsias, or live in an area where the atmosphere is too dry for these, investigate plants with these advantages: heat resistance, long bloom and color contrast. Whether your growing season is three months or year-round, annuals, herbaceous plants and small-growing shrubs will contribute variety in form, color and growth habits.

The following are some plants you are sure to find exciting to grow. Achimenes, gloxinia's cousin, will fill baskets for summer with season-long bloom. Either *Campanula fragilis* or *C.isophylla* are adapted to light shade. *Browallia* in deepest blue contrasts with *Schizanthus,* the "butterfly" flower that grows into a fall of myriad colors. *Convolvulus mauritanicus,* diminutive light blue morning glories and fragrant *Gardenia repens* are each shrubby in growth and do better in pots than moss-lined baskets. Several kinds of asparagus fern add cool green charm to an otherwise hot area. The polypodium ferns are unexcelled for high hanging plants because they will grow out all over the basket, making a delightful ball of green.

In areas with dry atmosphere most of these are more easily grown than the tuberous begonias, and will add interesting contrast and variety to the hanging garden in any area.

Plan for outdoor living

As summer approaches with its long outdoor living season, you may recall your resolve to create more privacy in the garden. Consider which method you most desire and which will be in harmony with the general landscape plan and your house material, and also consider the cost of different kinds of construction.

Now consider the different aspects of stone walls, wooden fences, wire fencing and living screens of either hedges or informal shrubs. Choose vines with small stem structures to cover wire fences. The jasmines and bignonias along with evergreen *Clematis armandii* have tendril and twining habits of growth that recommend them for covering both wooden and wire fences. Boston ivy and deciduous *Clematis* rank high in the deciduous group with hardiness as an ideal for colder regions. Bougainvillea and climbing roses are typical of heavy woody growth. Choose plants to be in character with the garden to enhance the overall effect.

Annual vines planted now will give shade this summer. *Cobaea scandens* (cup-and-saucer vine) spring up quickly

These deciduous *Clematis* are among the showiest of any vines, with a well-deserved popularity almost everywhere. Should be given partial shade in southern exposure. Photo by Charles Potter.

from seed, and become short-lived perennials. Cut them to the ground and mulch for winter protection where needed. Do the same with deciduous *Clematis,* and provide shade for the roots in warm latitudes. The delicate tracery of vines is to the garden what grace notes are to music.

Score card to judge hedge plants

These points may be helpful when choosing hedge plants: branching habit, leaf size and response to pruning. Plants that do not break freely at buds on their stems are unsuited to hedges. Meyer dwarf lemon and other bush citrus make admirable wide bush-type hedges, and if care is used in pruning considerable fragrance and fruit may be enjoyed. Also for near frost-free areas, *Carissa grandiflora* (Natal plum) grows into an impenetrable six-foot hedge. Trimming does not interfere with fruiting. Pyracantha is comparable and hardy to several degrees of frost. The *Mahonia aquifolium* (Oregon grape) is handsome in foliage, flower and fruit.

Some large-growing shrubs for screening where space is not a premium are pink oleander and *Plumbago capensis.* These thrive on heat, poor soil and moderate moisture, and flower all summer. Although they may get some frost damage at temperatures below 26° F., when spring returns they can be pruned back beyond frost damage for a fine summer display. *Plumbago* should be pruned harshly in any event. Work out old stems to the soil level.

These are but a few suggestions for vines and shrubs. For those that are favorites or enured to the hardships of your area visit nurseries, arboretums and botanic gardens in your region to see varieties to make your garden special.

Perfume for the night

Night-blooming plants with fragrance are legendary, but when we come to look for specific flowers they seem to be rare and scarce. When you plan the flowers for summer outdoor living areas also consider white and pastel color flowers and those with delicate lacy foliage that are complimented by artificial light.

These should be readily available: petunia, moonvine, *Nicotiana alata, Bouvardia humboldtii, Stephanotis flori-bunda,* and *Cestrum parqui* or *nocturnum.* The last are not attractive until the white fruits develop (and then are favored by flower arrangers), and the perfume is so heady they should be planted a distance from the outside sitting place. Most of these open in late afternoon or early evening to enhance the pleasant hours spent under the stars. We have been amused and delighted by the fragile butter-yellow four-petal blooms of evening primrose which explode dramatically for the dinner hour. Large sphinx moths come to extract nectar from the opening blooms and add motion to the otherwise quiet atmosphere.

Whether you choose fragrant flowers, scented foliage or both to add perfume to the garden, these few plants may be a springboard to further research. Diosma's small sharp-pointed leaves are so daintily fragrant that when translated the name means divine fragrance or breath of heaven. The white flower kind, *alba,* is the finer plant. Scented-leaf geraniums are an often neglected source of outdoor perfume, but for nostalgia *Lippia citriodora* (lemon verbena) and English lavender can't be equaled.

Just-for-fun gardening

Let me tell you about our pleasure and success with growing hummingbird feeders. While our neighbors are fussing with filling hummers' feeders we enjoy their visits to different bright flowers. Because there are several kinds of red-hot pokers (*Kniphofia*), some may be in bloom most of the summer. We place toothpicks in the stems for perches as the flowers begin to open. As the flower stems lengthen we raise the toothpick perches, thereby enjoying a longer visit. While these are certainly preferred by the acrobatic speeders, they will also visit most gay tubular blossoms.

Early summer pruning and cutting back gives plenty of slips for new plants. A potting bench or table in a shady place will make it possible to propagate many new plants. Softwood cuttings of such perennials as penstemon, carnation and chrysanthemums root readily, and often bloom that same season. New wood growth of shrubs is firm enough for cuttings by mid-June. With a home propagation center favorite colors and kinds of plants may be perpetuated to replace those becoming old and woody, to extend the planting, to share with friends, and for garden ,club plant exchanges or sales. Plastic bags tied over pots hasten rooting.

Check to see if plants are alive and well

Go over newly planted as well as established roses to see if the "eyes" you pruned to are growing. Otherwise cut canes down to buds that have begun to grow. This will prevent dieback traveling down the stem, which might cause the loss of the cane.

Use restraint in cutting flower stems from newly planted roses because leaves are needed to nourish the plant the first year in the garden. Remedial pruning can be done when cutting the first luscious blooms of the season. After the first flush of spring roses, it may be a month before a second bloom. This brief rest no doubt earned the term "monthly" for the early hybrid teas.

Balance moisture supply with food. Set up a regular feeding schedule and pay particular attention to fungi and chewing insects. Aphids will be fewer as summer sets in, but chewing creatures will be plentiful.

Roses—queens of the garden year

Seedsmen have developed cut-and-grow-again stock. By careful management we may enjoy much the same performance in the rose garden, but a cut-and-grow-again behavior can be a summer-long process only if care is used in cutting each bloom, in thoughtful pest control, and in watering and feeding.

One of the cardinal sins of rose growing is breaking off the fading flowers with the fingers. Clip off flowers with mini-shears or utility scissors and use judgment and consideration when you do. If you must gather fading petals to prevent littering the garden paths or beds, merely pull them off; leave the calyx for a time when you have shears and a container to put it in. In this way you will also have an abundance of flowers to dry for potpourri. After all the blooms on a stem have faded, cut the stem back to at least pencil-size wood to a leaf node where growth buds will be found. These "eyes" develop new branches on which successive flowers will grow.

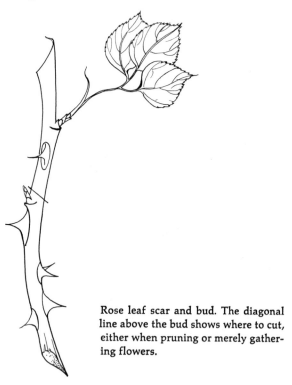

Rose leaf scar and bud. The diagonal line above the bud shows where to cut, either when pruning or merely gathering flowers.

There are at least three types of rose growers: the purist who never cuts a rose, because its destiny must be fulfilled in a seed which is contained in the rose hip or haw; the nervous gardener who can't stand to see petals on the ground and goes about the garden snapping off fading flowers; and the practical gardener who learns the habits of various rose types, gives them the best location in the garden, and follows through with seasonal care.

Here is rose care routine that will ensure high production. With warmer days and lush foliage aphids and mildew may reach a maximum infestation. Use a nozzle to make a strong force of water, and hose down the plants each morning for control of these destructive insects and diseases. Water deeply every week on light soil during drought, less frequently on heavy soils. Use this as a guide, not a rule. In addition to the hosing down use a dual-purpose spray occasionally. Feed plants monthly with a cupful of a complete plant food, geared to the chemical reaction of your soil, remembering roses grow best with an analysis of slightly below pH 7 which is normal (see chapter 6).

Use a numbers game as an aid in season-long care of established roses. Number the stems or branches. The plant you begin with after winter pruning, or a new rose just planted, is *number one*. The first strong wood growth which will produce the exuberant spring bloom is *number two,* and the second flowering wood is *number three*. It is these last two that become the working wood that is cut back during summer to give long-stemmed flowers for bouquets and for garden color. Seldom cut back number one before early autumn renovation, or under extreme weather conditions, perhaps not even then.

Cut this year's planted roses more lightly than older bushes. They need leaves to nourish the newly transplanted bushes. Don't be disappointed if the new roses in your garden do not measure up to AARS committee standards in either plant vigor or flower beauty. The second year in the garden will tell whether the variety is planted in the right location, the kind of soil and other conditions that could easily influence the quality. Visit municipal rose gardens to discover how gorgeous the new roses will be when the plants are established.

Learn to recognize tell-tale signs

Curling of new leaves can be caused by aphids. Soft mounds of well-tilled soil may mean gophers nest-building in the roots of nearby choice shrubs. A flash of gold across the sky marks the return of orioles. A noisy chatter from a shrub announces a house wren's presence and reminds us that a nest box can ensure nearby automated pest control.

It isn't too early to make and put nest boxes for summer

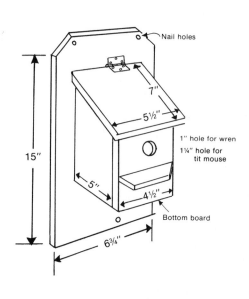

Rustic or man-made nest boxes add sound and movement to a garden. You can count the frequent insect offerings the busy wrens make by the brief song they make on each trip which continues from earliest morning until complete darkness. The unique entrance hole of this rustic nest box is an attempt of nature to heal an area where a branch was broken. These interesting bits of "drift wood" make charming bird houses. But if a more conventional nest box blends better with your garden furnishings the plan shown here will be acceptable, and an easy workbench project.

resident birds. Wrens and titmice, in particular, will stay in your garden if housing is provided, ensuring on-the-spot control of pests, aphids and all manner of worms. Since they are entirely insect- and seed-eating birds, we do not hesitate to make inviting places for them to raise their young in comparative safety.

Allow from four to six weeks from the time the birds choose the housing you have provided before young brood will be hatched. This will coincide with the high tide of summer chewing and sucking insects. In areas where purple martins live the multiple housing units are a picturesque feature of gardens.

The cause and effect of pest control is worthy of every

gardener's consideration. Which outweighs the other depends upon your skill and devotion to detail. For instance, if on your early morning rounds you see a silvery trail where snails and/or slugs have gone, and do nothing about it, the effect will be eaten plants.

Ants trailing up tree trunks generally mean scale or aphid infestation. To neglect control may mean the loss of valuable trees. Use oil emulsion spray on trees, and track ants to their nests. Dispatch them there with a specific control.

Earth and air insects

About now wooly aphids may appear on pyracantha, apple and other firm-wooded plants. They come forth from winter earth hibernation to breed. Rough tobacco stems and chaff piled at the base of plants often act as an effective deterrent against these difficult-to-control insects. This inexpensive mulch, not available everywhere, is also efficient pest control on rose beds.

Ant traffic in the garden is an indication of scale or aphids on plants. Ants feed on the honeydew excreted by these sucking insects. For ant control, impregnate cotton batten with ant poison and form into bands to fasten around plant stems and tree trunks to prevent ant traffic that spreads the infestation to other areas of the garden. Then go after the scale and aphids in earnest with suitable formulas, and the ants, too (see chapter 6).

It is good time conservation to use a dual-purpose spray, since both aphids and mildew may be present. After two or three days look to see what success the spray may have had.

Summer brings flowers. Harriet Foster tends baskets of geraniums that brighten her outdoor living areas. Inspiration for planting in containers is found in Chapter 6.

Chapter 2
Summer

"All green and fair the summer lies,
Just budded from the land of spring
With tender blue of wistful skies,
and winds which softly sing."

Susan Coolidge

June

This month summer turns the corner and brings the longest day of the year. Gardeners' hopes run high, and as coworkers with nature we need to cultivate a sensitivity to her whims. Only a carefully arranged schedule will help to keep up with the activity and still allow leisure to enjoy the garden you work to make.

June is a month of firsts: the first splendid roses, the first delicious garden-fresh summer fruits and vegetables, the first of a long season of giving plants supplemental water. Establish a regular routine of garden chores which if begun now will avoid a frenzy of work later in the summer.

Gardening is the threshold to an absorbing new world where we learn not only about plants but the earth in which they grow, which kinds do well together, where they grow best, and those that are hardy or delicate, good to eat, pleasant to smell, or attractive to insects. This is an exhilarating world of open air, high adventure and sometimes complete failure, but also of good stout courage.

Arithmetic for gardeners

You don't need a computer to program your plants' growth responses. Your five senses will give the answers. Look at their general well-being. Hear insects at work. Smell the fragrance of earth and flowers. Taste leaves and fruit to judge the response to fertilizers. Touch leaves to see if there is enough soil moisture to keep them crisp so the plant can carry on photosynthesis.

Although the summer solstice which brings the longest day of the year is pinpointed at the two-thirds mark of June, the process of lengthening days is too subtle to perceive, just as it is not possible to sense the gradually shortening days until we are well toward the end of summer. The enjoyment we get from any season depends upon our location, activity and point of view. If you tend to be lazy, summer is not for you. We may look in vain for those "long lazy days of June." However, it is a delightful season for gardeners.

Coordinate your work

Like the mockingbird's song, summer chores are repeated again and again. For this reason, it is best to project them over the month when we enjoy long days, rather than to think of them separately. Coordinating different parts of the garden with the days of the week, such as Monday/Wednesday/Friday areas and Tuesday/Thursday/Saturday regions may prove a workable regime and keep most folks up-to-date on all parts of the garden. A further organization of the year's chores may be divided into seasonal needs of plants, which tends to simplify the work program still further. This I have hoped to accomplish in the four seasonal sections of this text (see The Orbit, page 8).

For this quarter-year you may revel and delight in outdoor activity, unless you overburden yourself with needless routine. Each season brings its peculiar chores. Summer warmth and rapid plant growth make demands upon moisture supply; bugs and fungi try the patience; rabbits above ground and gophers below command attention.

Continue summer routine

As summer advances, the need to shelter newly set plants may be lessened by prehardening them to open garden conditions and by careful planting. Nursery-bought seedlings are often held under lath for several days and become soft. Keep in half-sun for a few days to harden up tissues to stand more sun and warmth. Be sure to set plants in holes previously filled with water which has been allowed to seep away. Use a plant shelter for a few days to filter air and sun. A square of burlap with two wire supports to stick into the soil slantwise is a favorite for individual plants. Portable lath frames on foot-high stakes are more satisfactory for beds of plants like vegetables.

Eternal vigilance is the price we pay for an enjoyable garden. Continue planting heat-loving vegetables. Small but frequent plantings mean high yield and less pest control of cucumbers, squash, beans and corn. Zinnias and cosmos are two star performers. Goldfinch will frequent the garden when cosmos seed begin to set, lending their musical whispers to the garden.

Prevent rot and insect damage to eggplant and peppers by snipping off the lower branches to keep the fruit well off the ground. As plants gain height, tie the main stem loosely to a $^3/_4$ x $^3/_4$-inch stake with soft string.

An airy burlap sun shield will protect transplanted seedlings while they are getting over the shock of being moved.

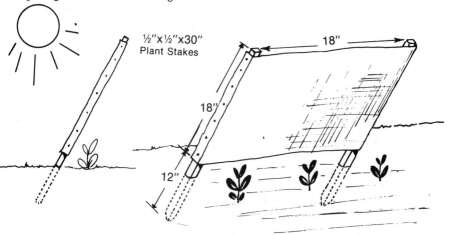

½"x½"x30"
Plant Stakes

18"

18"

12"

A mallow (cheese weed) may appear in odd places. It is a host plant to rust and fungi, which may infect the asparagus planting, beans and other plants susceptible to rust.

Handle insecticides with care

Right plant—wrong spray? Chemicals can cause plant allergies. Stop long enough to read the label on spray or dust packages. Be sure the plants you are to spray have a tolerance for the chemicals. Cucurbits (squash, cucumbers, etc.) are allergic to sulfur. Violets and most ferns may be seriously damaged by nicotine sulfate (Blackleaf 40). Plants' compatibility to exposure—sun, shade, soil type, food moisture and spray elements—should be taken into account before planting them together in the garden.

With summer pests, think double—earth and foliage. Snail, slug, and sowbug control is essential to keep the leaf garden whole and to protect flowers, fruit and vegetables from being ruined. Greenhorn worm and other temper-trying summer chewing monsters that have been star boarders should be seen less as days shorten. The hornworm larva hibernate in the hospitable soil until next spring's warmth brings forth the elegant sphinx moth from the curious brown chrysalids. Keep a watchful eye for all manner of pupa cases in the soil, rolled in leaves, or attached to leaf stems by delicate membranes. They can be used for nature study by your local school or disposed of for first-hand control of next summer's chewing insects.

During this transition month discard winter-spring plants and concentrate on those of summer. Rooting out plants has two advantages—pest control and higher production. Seasonal varieties are not only more in keeping with the time of year, but give higher returns.

Mildew, rust and thrips infest most aging vegetables, and in the flower garden calendulas, snapdragon, sweet pea and stock are also insect and fungi incubators. Because sowbugs often live in the friable soil around cabbage and broccoli roots, a specific control should be in the tool basket to use as soon as these plants are dug out (see chapter 6).

"Take time" is a magic formula

Despite modern scientific systemics and other miracle pesticides, the home gardener who is neither a chemist nor a seer is still in a quandry about how to combat the several kinds of chewing and sucking insects and mildew and rust. Read the labels on both the chemicals at hand and those on the nursery shelves. Summer warmth favors the appearance of a multiplicity of pests. Timing is the key to successful control. Tardy setting of plants may be overcome to some extent with extra rations of plant food, but fungi, insects and rodents aren't going to take a nap while we dilly-dally with their control.

Insects are rapacious. Take advantage of cool mornings to hand-pick the big ones which may continue to feed in full view. Enlist your own or friends' children in this "big game hunt." A bonus of a penny per snail, slug or greenhorn worm will lessen plant damage and create a lasting friendship between experienced gardener and youngsters.

Vacation help with garden

If children are with you during vacation, give them a small plot for their own to grow whatever they like. To lessen their

This easily constructed insect-catching net will aid in insect control, and be an intriguing companion to summer visitors.

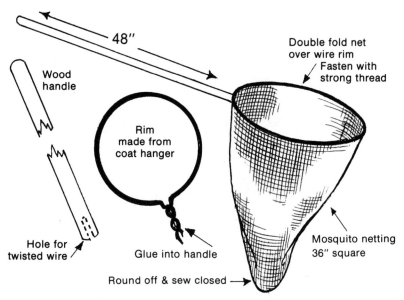

impatience plant things that are quick to come up, eager to grow and continue to yield: radishes, beans and squash to eat, and robust marigolds and zinnias to add charm and color to the garden.

When a child is old enough to do the planting himself he will learn what "follow through" means and that plants are living things which need food and water, above all else. He will learn friend from foe in the insect world. A garden is a complete biology lab. To encourage interest in this field help to make an insect-catching net. Simple directions are pictured here. A net will not only add to the young gardener's fun but prevent chewing insect larva from eating his (and your) plants, and may be the beginning of a life-long hobby and deep interest in the natural world. He will learn the difference between the green twelve-spot cucumber beetle and the beneficial ladybird beetle and how to tell the lacewing katydid from the helpful praying mantis.

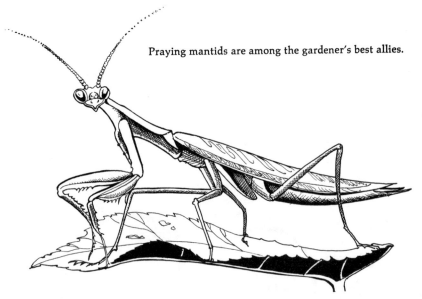

Praying mantids are among the gardener's best allies.

Plant care after harvest

Asparagus harvest is past. The delicious, succulent stalks of spring give way to tall branching stems which by mid-summer may be four feet high and fill the bed. Because this growth should be left until it ripens in autumn, it may be advisable to surround the bed with string tied to stakes at the corners to prevent this vegetation from lopping over the paths.

An occasional application of a complete vegetable dust will control the blue and red beetle and rust. Dress the bed in mid-summer with a complete plant food and a light application of wood ash or lime to keep the soil alkaline.

Avoid surpluses

Harvest of fruits, flowers and vegetables is exciting, but time consuming. An oversupply of any one of these can be frustrating. Surpluses may be avoided by planned planting, and by canning, freezing or drying the abundance. Learn how to determine the length of row or number of plants. Take squash as an example; these lush vines bear continuously and abundantly for about three weeks. A few plants renewed frequently for high performance will give best results. One hill of three popular kinds will produce so many squash that your family may rebel, no matter how ingenious your recipes. Plant leaf lettuce and heading kinds at the same time. The leaf lettuce will be harvested before the heading varieties mature.

Quality, texture and the time of year fruits ripen may be used as a clue to successful fruit culture. Spring-ripening berries, being high in moisture and maturing quickly, need copious amounts of food and water. Figs and grapes, on the other hand, will split open and spoil if given too much water, and being hot-weather fruits, need high temperatures to reach perfection. Summer peaches, plums and apricots are not to be watered after the pits are hard, until the fruit is harvested—three weeks to a month.

Harvest gourmet quality

Make the most of summer; become a harvest connoisseur. During these mid-year long days and warm evenings maintenance is the magic touch that keeps the garden gay, healthful and productive. Water early and tidy late is good routine. Keep fading flowers clipped and plants well supported. Most gathering can be done after the shadows have lengthened. Learn to judge prime quality. The silk of corn should be crisp; squash and cucumber seed should be tender, after a bean can be shelled its best flavor is gone and it is much too old for the freezer. Most flowers should be cut before full-blown and placed in large containers of cold water for arranging at your leisure. This is a delightful late afternoon task.

These are the tangible rewards we can touch, taste and smell. The intangible items of harvest are best expressed by poets, but all of us may enjoy the beauty of form and color and delight of a summer breeze. The long-growing hours when the shortening length of days is not yet apparent are best for gathering a bountiful harvest.

Timing is the clue

When to plant and when to harvest; when to water and when to feed; when to prune and when to spray? A rule of thumb is: when flowers begin to bloom, plant for the next season; when vegetables are ready to harvest, replant, not necessarily the same kind, because different varieties and even kinds change with the seasons. Winter peas will follow summer beans. Make new plantings of tomato and pepper, zucchini squash and bush wax beans for autumn harvest, rather than hold onto summer-weary plants.

Take time to stake plants before they topple over. Use various kinds, sizes and shapes of supports. Take time to thin seedlings, which is good advice any time. Flower seedlings grow rapidly, radishes may crowd each other out of the ground, carrots twist about each other and lettuce leaves turn brown if allowed to grow too thickly. Summer is the hightide of harvest. Color is rampant, outdoor living is being enjoyed by families working and playing together. Deep satisfaction comes from growing thrifty productive plants from seed sown in mellow soil, or starting flourishing slips to embellish our borders.

Rotate crops for soil health

Because we are nearing autumn and replanting will be the order of the day, this is a good time to make plans for rotating crops for better soil and plant health. By planting different kinds of crops soil fertility is increased and diseases lessened. Legumes are good soil builders and will add nitrogen to the soil that is used by nonlegume plants, like roots and lettuce. Peas and beans in great variety may be grown over a long season. This small table may help you to understand how to go about rotation over a three-year period, after which you begin all over.

	Area 1	Area 2	Area 3
1st year	Roots	Lettuce, etc.	Peas, beans, celery, leeks
2nd year	Peas, beans, celery, leeks	Roots	Lettuce, etc.
3rd year	Lettuce, etc.	Peas, beans, celery, leeks	Roots

July

This is the time of roses because these summer beauties need warmth for perfection of bloom. Other flowers and plants also begin their fulfillment this second month of summer. The ebb and flow of the growth cycle reaches tidal rhythms with the season. After flood tide it will be a long time until the ebbing due to the long summer growing season.

Drought may be just around the corner

Beware of approaching drought. Natural moisture from winter rains diminishes rapidly through evaporation, by the growth of plants and by seepage into surrounding soil. Replace the deficit before plants suffer. The big demand for applied water by hose, ditch or other method is urgent. To encourage new roots of recently planted balled in burlap citrus and avocado trees, trickle water slowly about once a week near the stem of the tree.

Plastic seeper hoses do a thorough job of soil soaking, and overhead sprinkling benefits many plants, but may cause blossom-end rot of young squash by waterlogging the blooms. When watering with sprinklers be careful to make the sets so as to prevent mist being carried onto plants not being watered. Otherwise, salts may coat over the leaf surfaces and seriously interfere with their function. This reaction is particularly noticeable on days of extremely low humidity when the mist dries quickly and may easily be mistaken for leaf burn attributed to sun shining on wet foliage.

Continuous color display is a challenge

To provide continuous garden color through the year is a challenge. Plants to face a path are scarce, but these well-behaved ones have given me real joy: *Nierembergia* 'Purple Robe,' *Convolvulus mauritanicus, Nepeta mussinii, Potentilla parryi,* and violets in variety. They all combine compact growth, long flowering and good color with pleasing contrast in foliage and flower form. Planted now they will give a path edging genuine charm.

Bulb flowers add an extra touch to borders. Small-flowered kinds brighten a pathway when they flower and since many will bloom before the perennials, they lengthen the seasonal color parade. Large-flowered bulbs planted between and behind clumps of perennials give a lift to flagging color displays. The perplexing drying bulb foliage may be tucked under expanding perennials. This is especially good placement for *Amaryllis belladonna* and other bulbs that bloom without foliage.

Although bulbs with evergreen foliage require some maintenance—removal of old leaves and flower stalks that were not cut for bouquets—when dressed with a complete plant food, they will make an interesting contrast to the border with grass-like foliage. As summer advances you may resolve to set aside a place where plants can be heeled in to ripen. An alternate plan is to hide the maturing bulb foliage among herbaceous perennials that may be used as companion plants.

Now is a good time to decide if the fleeting color of glads is worthwhile. They have been developed to a point that the heavy flower stalks need staking and they should be lifted after each flowering for best control of thrips. Spuria iris, on the other hand, requires less maintenance and is graceful in flower arrangements, so when contrasted with glads, a busy gardener may choose spuria iris.

Grow a challenging plant

Have cascade chrysanthemums interested you but seemed too fussy? Actually, they are quite simple and give a wonderful sense of accomplishment. Colorful curtains of bloom may decorate a planter, accent a shelf or spill from a hanging pot or basket. Like other growing techniques there are shortcuts. For example, plants may be grown in earth beds through August, if that is easier, before potting up, but training is begun now.

Choose a plant with limber stems and close-set leaf nodes. Allow plants to reach twelve inches in height. Pinch the tips to encourage branching. Keep three to five stems, depending upon the fullness of the mature plant you want. At this point make the training frame according to the diagram shown.

As main stems grow, tie them to the frame at close intervals. Set the frame near the plant. Keep side shoots pinched to encourage bushy growth, but allow the main stems

It is exciting to grow something that is a challenge, yet easily within our skill as gardeners. In place of the wire training frame shown here, one may be made of small boughs. Young growth of willow, or other pliant branches will lend themselves to bending. Excellent directions will be found in this chapter.

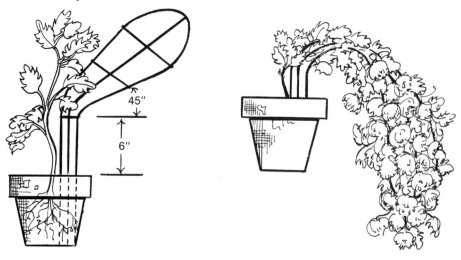

to grow. Gradually bend the wire frame to cascade position and try to keep the plant off the ground. Use liquid plant food each month and plenty of water. These plants may also be trained over driftwood and create an aged tree effect.

Dahlias for sun

Dahlias are to the sun garden what begonias are to shaded areas. For good keeping, cut the flowers in late afternoon, crush the stem ends and plunge into cold water up to their necks. Let soak overnight and arrange the next day.

Disbud both dahlias and chrysanthemums that are being grown for display of prize-winning blooms as they begin to develop buds. Because of the rigid one-stake-to-a-stem method of growing these handsome large flowers they are usually not grown in the garden for display, but in areas such as the vegetable garden.

If you have an area to display golden glow and cannas, you won't lack for summer background color. Tree dahlias, either *imperialis* or *maxonii*, give profuse white or lavender flowers in late summer and lend graceful charm and high color. Provide stakes.

Plan ahead

To paraphrase an old adage, "a snip in time saves nine" certainly applies to chrysanthemums. Don't just pinch off the terminal buds, but shorten stems back to at least fourteen inches. In August keep an additional four inches of height when you cut back the plants. I also advocate early staking of chrysanthemums. Two oft-repeated errors are too few stakes and starting too late. Stake the plants as they develop new stem growth. Use several light-weight stakes placed to follow the branch line and begin lacing raffia or strong string through the plants to form a basket effect and to prevent breaking over. This is particularly important as autumn storms approach.

Narcissus bulbs that failed to bloom last season should be reset before autumn growth begins. Enrich the soil with either bonemeal or super-phosphate. Top-dress bulb beds annually with a complete plant food that is high in this element, such as 5–10–5.

Divide iris and discard the old rhyzomes; trim the leaves to an inverted V, which not only reduces transpiration while new foots are forming, but prevents emerging new leaves from having the tops cut off as happens when the old leaves are cut square.

As soon as delphinium stalks complete flowering, cut them down, mulch with manure, and water thoroughly. If the soil was prepared with leaf mold or peat moss, a light dressing of lime or wood ash may bring better second bloom. Meanwhile, the new soft gray-green foliage will be decorative.

Plant cool colors

Cool down the garden, at least visually, with gray foliage, white and pastel colored flowers and living ground-cover plants. The daily display of massed flowers and pleasing foliage add up to garden beauty and minimum care.

Hybrid tea and floribunda roses will take a rest unless their food supply is met and care is used in clipping fading flowers. As flowers fade, cut hybrid tea back to pencil-size wood and floribundas to a plump viable eye or bud.

Along with these suggestions for the delight of the summer garden, I want to recommend these few splendid ornamental small fruit trees, each with a distinct personality. Least known—the jujube—makes a narrow bright green summer-leafing tree. Quince and pomegranate need no introduction, only a bit of urging for their inclusion in the patio or garden. Both make large handsome tub plants. White fruiting figs form impressive screening when trained on a trellis.

Harvest is an important aspect of this long-day season that calls for frequent feeding to maintain high production, proper pest control and (of course) watering and replanting. We shouldn't expect any annual—flower or vegetable—to give peak performance all summer long. The trick is to plant perennials that give as much color as annuals and bloom when those are spent.

Toward the end of this month new seeds of perennials will be available. Sow in boxes and set in coolish half-shade; the young plants will reach pricking-out size quickly, be ready for open ground planting this fall, and bloom the following

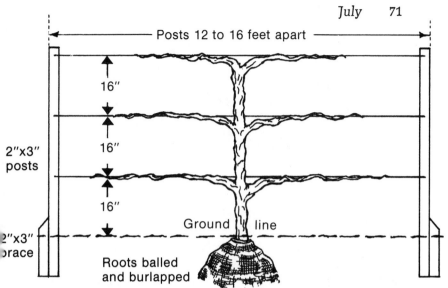

This sturdy garden trellis may be used for many training jobs; espaliering trees, berry and/or grape vines.

summer. Starting plants from seed is not only an inexpensive way to get new plants, but is often the only way if the variety is new, rare, or if wanted in separate colors.

Planting for late summer abundance

Are annual flower and vegetable plants star performers in your garden or merely boàrders? If frost is uncommon or much delayed in your area, new tomato plants will outdo old summer-weary ones. Replant with small-fruited, more hardy kinds.

At month's end sow seed of wax beans and peas. Seed of root vegetables will germinate readily. The cut-and-grow-again feature of broccoli makes it the most rewarding of the cabbage family. Contrive a covering of mosquito netting to thwart the small cabbage butterfly that produces the troublesome worms, and the lyrical white crown sparrow that finds the foliage quite tasty.

Grow onions, chives and leek nearby for genuine seasoning enjoyment and to aid in aphid control. Remember to freeze and/or ovendry parsley and chives to use during late summer and early winter when these delectable herbs are resting. Any of the alliums may be planted where leeks are mentioned. However, we have found these mild onions not only of the easiest culture, but real fun. These and chives are a continuous crop if some seed heads are allowed to ripen.

Get a headstart on next spring's growth by planting citrus and avocado trees now. Warm soil encourages root growth and often saves a season's growth.

Be aware of the beauty of summer

The enjoyment of our gardens can be greatly enhanced by being aware of the summer beauty around us. With the sight of color and the play of light and shade over the garden; the sound of wind, the rustle of bamboo, or the splash of water in a fountain; the touch of leaf textures and cool green grass beneath our feet; the smell of flower perfume and moist earth after a shower; and the taste of herb leaves, spicy old-fashioned pinks and rose petals, our five senses are given full play. Some of these pleasures can be further increased by bringing flowers indoors during the heyday of bloom. Fixing flowers is a relaxed way of enjoying the beauty and bounty of our land.

Consider the art and craft of gardening

Husbandry is an old-fashioned word that spells out the art and craft of gardening, but since we cannot wave a magic wand or by wishful thinking accomplish the daily routine of maintaining a garden, we need a carefully calculated schedule to fit various chores into a workable, enjoyable program. Sequence of work may be the secret—dry chores should be done before beginning to water, prune before feeding. Experience should make chores easier and yields greater if we observe the results and jot down our mistakes and successes. A garden record is the best "memory" a gardener can have. To encourage record keeping use the detailed sheets placed at the end of the book.

Tradition does not always work out

Winter is considered as traditional pruning time. However, there is leaf-time pruning to do now. Deciduous spring-flowering shrubs and trees that give gardens a breathtaking festival quality should be trimmed now to encourage new wood growth that will repeat the seasonal display next spring. Syringa, spiraea, cut-leaf Persian lilac, flowering quince and almond are a few shrubs, and the gay flowering-fruiting trees represent dual-purpose plants.

Another phase of green-wood pruning that is beginning to be accepted is pruning of almost all plants, especially newly planted trees. The extra light and air that recently set-out plants enjoy over crowded nursery conditions releases and provides abundant vigor. Buds that may have remained dormant burst forth with robust growth.

Only a watchful eye will prevent such pent-up energy from making too much growth. To keep the plant in balance, pinch out the terminal buds before the new stems have gained much length. By such careful pinching we can direct this energy to all parts of the plant and often achieve not only better-shaped trees, but lessen by at least 75 percent the surplus wood that will need to be pruned off. Nor is this the only advantage: by this technique a larger, permanent structure is grown. The plant can actually grow as much in one season as it could in two years under the older method of culture when the plant was allowed to grow willy-nilly.

(You don't have to be a soil scientist to discover soil deficiencies which show up by late summer in slowing growth, anemic-looking leaves and a falling off in production. It may be late in the year to correct this condition, but a complete plant food with a 6–10–6 formula will improve the general health of ailing plants. Neglecting to apply replenishing foods in autumn is an error I frequently encounter.)

The enjoyment of watering

Irrigation is as refreshing to the gardener as to the garden. Water wands arch gracefully above field and grove and smaller sprinklers bring invigorating humidity to the atmosphere, crispness to foliage and moisture to the parched earth. Shrub areas may be landscaped with drought-enduring plants, but flowers and vegetables require high moisture to complete their growth cycle. Because many plants are at maximum growth now, the demand for water is heavy. This can be the driest month of the year, bringing the biggest water bill, and may also mean maximum soil alkalinity. Whether you are short of water for irrigation or just plain thrifty, sprinkler application is practical because it has been found that two and one-half times less water is needed as in flooding or furrow irrigation. Other advantages of sprinkling are less soil compaction with better seed germination and plant growth, and less salt concentration on the soil surface that forms a crust causing young seedlings to die off at the ground.

Drying out of soil of camellias may cause bud drop. This month and next may be the driest of the year. Keep ornamental and fruit trees that were planted this year well watered. It may be late for plant food to help deciduous plants, but evergreens will respond and the new wood growth will mature before frost.

Because warmth and moisture favor the growth of oakroot fungus (*Armillaria mellea*), summer watering of live oaks should be kept to a minimum. A garden under these spendid native trees should be landscaped with great care to avoid this danger. Plants grown in containers, or stones or brick paving laid in porous grout rather than living ground covers are two ideas to lessen the amount of watering.

Maintenance is the trump card

Perpetual maintenance is the key to continued production. This includes adequate but not wasteful use of plant foods and frequent applications of pest control material. Pinhead-sized snails as well as those an inch wide will come forth to feed on tender foliage, climbing tree trunks to feast on leaves. Use bait for these and begin dusting against powdery mildew as soon as new squash and cucumber plants emerge. This fungi is the foe of many plants in a summer-dry climate.

Integrate the pest control. A hit-and-miss application will not give superior results. Sprays and dusts are used as prevention and control and are economical if used wisely. Go over all insecticides now to see what you have on hand, and what you may need for the upcoming autumn garden plants.

A flyswatter-size paddle on a two-foot handle is a good device for grasshopper extermination. Most "monsters" are easily hand-picked and if dropped into a gathering bag may be included with other gleanings of the day for disposal. While manual methods are effective, they may not be practical for complete control over a large area or where population is extensive. In these cases use a potent stomach poison, in both bait and spray form (see chapter 6).

Get to know your garden friends

However, the insect world is not one-sided. Nature showers us with good insects, too. Consider these few: ladybird beetles destroy plant lice and scale; hornets feed almost entirely on insects; spiders eat flies and small moths; and wasps not only eat insects but feed them to their larva in their intricate nests. Dragonflies hover in the air, catching mosquitoes and gnats. Frogs and toads go after slugs; lizards live on small beetles and worms. These are a few of our garden friends. Learn to recognize them, encourage them and protect them by using only nonpoisonous sprays and dusts.

Rodent control will be relatively easy because both the troublesome ground squirrel that carries off succulent vegetables and the gourmand pocket gopher that pulls choice plants down his burrow will take poisoned grain readily. Place it well into the tunnels out of the reach of birds. Rodents die underground so pets will not find their carcasses. Yet another effective control for gophers is a trap line. Learn kinds that are most effective and where to place them, and the technique of setting traps. Poisons and traps together will work better than either method alone (see chapter 6).

August

August brings the full ripeness of the year. Plants tumble over each other in exuberant growth, fruits burst forth with honeyed juices, vegetables crisp with quick maturity and flower colors are intensified by the sun's radiance. Many warm days are yet to come but days now are growing shorter, which sounds a warning of approaching autumn.

Even with its color and gaiety August can be frustrating unless we plan carefully, work diligently and look ahead. Plan now for the garden you will enjoy during late winter and early spring, and work to keep the present garden glowing.

A replanting time

August, like May, is a replanting time. Each month is a threshold to the season that is to come, particularly those that either begin or end a seasonal period. By month's end many annuals, both flower and vegetable, will have passed their high seasonal yield. It may be the last curtain call for several garden star performers as well as chores to be done. Annuals become weary and thrips-laden and make seed in spite of diligence.

Continue July maintenance work—pruning, spraying and feeding. Then add the later summer routine that develops with the advancing year. Even with this workload there is as much leisure as a gardener ever has.

Get new life into the garden with food, deep leaching with sprinkling, and light pruning. Roses will take a natural rest and bloom may diminish, but don't let this lethargy continue. Encourage new performance by carefully cutting out unproductive wood, and apply liquid plant food to encourage new wood growth for autumn flowers. Aside from the enjoyment an abundance of roses will bring is the bonus of blooms for late summer and autumn flower shows, reception teas for new teachers and club members, and house and garden color.

The revolutionary time of year

Summer months are revolutionary; tasks are completed and others begun. This is the last month to feed camellias, and unless kept moist they may drop their buds. Autumn-flowering Sasanqua camellias make a genuine contribution to garden color and form. Continue feeding perennials that will give color to the late summer and autumn garden. Maintain growth of all permanent plants by applying complete plant food. Choose the right formula for the type of plant.

Yellow leaves and marginal burn are especially prevalent following a dry winter because the accumulated salts of the past season's irrigation water were not leached out of the soil. Both symptoms appear after long periods of drought and continuous irrigation. To correct the condition use an acid-base plant food and iron, or use each element separately, because plants that do not require acid food may suffer from an iron deficiency. When broad-leafed evergreens show these maladies use both elements.

Since prevention is better than cure, use cottonseed meal as an all-purpose plant food for all plants that grow best with a light acid soil reaction. Frequent watering leaches nutrients below plants' roots, because nitrogen and potash move with soil moisture. Periodic light feeding of hill and row or border plants by side-dressing will pay big dividends in continued growth, rather than one big application at planting time.

For economy and maximum value from plant foods annuals should not be fed after flowering begins. Feed any plants that are not making satisfactory growth if other conditions of soil, moisture and exposure are good. This is the last month to feed azaleas, rhododendron, cymbidium orchids, and citrus and avocado trees.

A bloom for all seasons

Hydrangeas are summer star performers. Fed four times during the growing season and kept well watered, few plants can equal them for an elegant cool effect. Cut fading flowers much as you do roses, but save some for winter bouquets. Treated with glycerine, they remain pliable and become a soft bronze color. Make a solution of one-third glycerine and two-thirds water. Make enough to cover the bottom of a jar about two inches deep. Let the stems remain in the container until all the fluid has been absorbed.

Summer pruning is beneficial

Summer pruning produces long-lasting results. While the tree canopy still casts its cooling shade it is easy to determine where branch thinning and shortening will benefit the tree and also be desirable in the garden. Before beginning to cut, study the tree and mark the limbs you think should come out with streamers of cloth. Don't be in a hurry to prune, do a little at a time, and observe what effect each cut produces. Thinning branches of young trees should be done gradually. To remove too much of the leaf surface will deprive the tree of the food manufacturing the foliage produces. Small wounds will be healed quickly with the free-flowing sap.

Lightly prune broad-leafed evergreens and shape conifers. Control woody branches of deciduous fruit trees by cutting to a side branch—not to a bud. This is the last month to cut back garden-type chrysanthemums, after which they should be twelve to fourteen inches high. Keep watered well and feed monthly. Liquid manure is an excellent plant food (see chapter 7). If the plants become crowded move alternate clumps to control rust. Cut back carnations to induce new cutting wood for September. Practice plant renovation by cutting back woody perennials as they go out of bloom.

Cut back and tidy up English lavender plants. As the flower spikes mature, remove stems that bore only small flowers. Cut off all stems that are lying on the ground. As the bushes begin to separate in the middle tie them together with a band of strong cord. Face down the lavender with perennial catmint—*Nepeta mussinii*—a plant that can hardly be overpraised. After the first bloom is passed, about now, shear out the middle of the plants and side shoots will grow up and give second bloom. Slips root readily.

It is a good idea to prune poinsettias now. Remove from one-half to two-thirds of the new seasonal growth for bushy plants and more color and to lessen storm damage and the need for elaborate staking.

Consider the art of plant support

Here are two staking devices I've used and found not only adequate but inconspicuous enough to meet the high standard of the most aesthetic gardener. Bamboo supports for tall-growing flower spikes can be put up in sections as the growth warrants to avoid the forest of bare stakes so abhorred by discerning gardeners.

Because bamboo does not drive easily, use short lengths of pipe large enough to act as a socket for the first and larger bamboo. The support can be lengthened through a progression of sizes by slipping smaller sizes into the larger ones. Be careful to remove the top leaf node from each length; otherwise you will not have a hollow stem to receive the next section.

Perennial asters, tall-growing garden chrysanthemums and similar multistemmed plants that give splendid autumn mass color effects need special training devices. They should not be tied to a single stake, but rather supported by stiff-branching sprays of shrubbery. Thrust the butts of the boughs toward the base of the plant, under and among the stems, especially toward the front, which will give a natural and charming display without tying. This device also is effective for flowering shrubs that tend to lop over.

Staking plants can be lessened by good grooming. Only those with naturally weak stems and tall flower spikes should need either splints or crutches. Elaborate staking is not a substitute for good pruning and can otherwise mar beautiful effects.

Gourmand garden boarders

Most summer chewing insects have gourmand appetites. Rose slugs, like cucumber beetles and greenhorn tomato worms, do not confine their depredation to their namesake plants, but forage far and wide, from plum and pear foliage to zinnia and petunia.

Summer chewing insects feed mostly at dawn and dusk on succulent foliage. It may help to find them if their habits are known. Measuring worms make about a 1/4-inch swath each trip across a leaf. When the white cabbage butterfly comes flitting by, leaf damage will show up soon.When bug hunting look on the ground for fresh droppings, then in the foliage above for the diners.

In colder regions, big chewing "creatures" come forth to assuage their long hunger; in warm latitudes gardeners are plagued with snails, slugs, sow and pill bugs—not to forget earwigs—year-round.

Snails and slugs wear holes in leaves with sandpaper-like tongues. Most beetles eat holes or skeletonize leaves while others prefer rose buds. Ravenous grasshoppers tear off leaf parts in exchange for evening music. The greenhorn worms of the vegetable garden are children of the agile giant sphinx moths that nightly probe tubular blossoms for nectar.

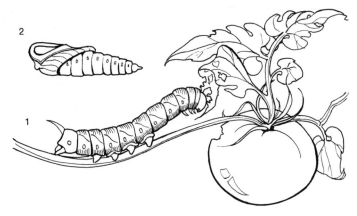

1.Larva   2. Pupa of green hornworm

The so-called "greenhorn" tomato worm is a summer boarder upon many plants of the solanum family. The curious pupa may be found when turning the warming soil in the spring.

To reap a continuous harvest apply plenty of food and water. Lush growth requires available nutrients. If the need is anticipated, organic plant foods may be used. Otherwise, chemical nitrogen will give failing plants a quick boost.

Save your homegrown mulches

Because mulches take a big bite out of the garden budget, conserve every particle of discarded plant material. Bean straw is an excellent source of minerals, and is relatively inexpensive in bean-growing areas. Lawn clippings make a porous mulch when dried lightly, except Bermuda grass, which should be composted before being used (see section on compost in chapter 7).

Although different in appearance, vegetable and mineral mulches accomplish about the same thing. Each has its place.

To be effective and in the spirit of the garden, mulches should be chosen with care. Dress plants with high-water needs with organic fibers. Peat moss, leaf mold and manure improve the garden's appearance, retain moisture by keeping the soil a more even temperature, lessen cultivation and help to control weeds.

Stone mulching is not new, but the vogue for its use in the garden is recent. This is one fad that makes common sense. Good examples may be studied in nature. An advantage of stone chips is their infinite variety in color and texture and their harmony with rock garden plants and others with low water needs. Stone chips can often be had for the taking from stream beds, beaches or mountain sides. Any mulch you can conserve or come by cheaply may leave that much cash for other needs of the garden.

Consider the technique of using stones in your garden. Aggregates up to two inches make a congenial hiding place for sowbugs, pillbugs or earwigs, and rocks from four to eight inches, when laid on top of the ground, are a perfect haven for them. However, large stones, because of their weight, are safe to use.

Keep in step with the season

Calendula may replace African marigolds. Stock and snapdragon will alter the color scheme. However, if long gaps are to be avoided in color or yield it will be necessary to do growing on. If you buy young plants, rather than begin with seed flats, spacing them further apart in boxes or in separate pots or plant bands will shorten the time between harvests. The rhythm of the season runs through the work program like a refrain with delightful crescendos and diminuendos of harvest, making summer one of the gayest times of the year.

Look your garden over

Take advantage of early day coolness to make changes in the garden landscape. To see if a plant fits your garden, weigh its total year-round performance, growth habits, ease of culture, long season of bloom and a bonus of perfume. Color and display may also add enjoyable dimensions. Choose plants that either retain most of their leaves, or whose leaves fall rapidly. Clipping fading flowers is time consuming and tedious. Also good are flowers that give high periodic bloom that may be shorn off, such as marguerites and the adaptable sweet alyssum.

Consider how leaves, flowers and fruit contribute to the overall beauty and use of various areas, or how they detract by staining walks, littering lawns and even creating a hazard with thorns or large succulent flowers on paths. *Solandra guttata* (cup-of-gold) and Burmese honeysuckle are excellent examples of fleshy blooms.

Late summer feasting

Melon time! These delicious foods need more time to come to harvest than most annuals we grow. Here are a few tips to ensure good eating whether they are homegrown or bought at a market. If melons are chilled the aroma will not be so pronounced, and you then use these tests for ripeness.

The skin on honeydew should feel waxy, and be cream-colored without a trace of green. The blossom end of any melon should be springy or soft to the touch when pressed gently, and the seed should rattle when the melon is shaken. Cantaloupe "netting" should be prominent and the skin yellow. A better test for ripeness of watermelons than the thump is a yellow patch on the upper round of the blossom end.

To grow top quality melons, limit vines to six or eight feet across. Fruit that sets further from the crown will not have time to mature, and will lack flavor and aroma.

To avoid wasting even one, protect melons from ground insects and gophers with platforms of four small slats to raise them off the ground. Small pieces of hardware cloth laid over the platform to eliminate ground contact will ensure perfect melons.

Growth insurance for another season

"Composted" manure is usually available at plant stores. Where space permits old-fashioned gardeners may prefer to do their own and save money on plant food. Gauge the amount you compost to the size garden you have. It will be a substantial growth factor in the fall garden. Calcium added before composting will enhance the value and lessen the odor. Make the pile flattish on top, after the manner of conventional compost piles. Water well, and when heat begins to develop, toss it over once, and soon it will be ready to use on almost any plant. Then stand back and watch the new growth. Camellias especially will respond to this organic dressing. Liquid manure will also be a great booster. Make this potent plant tea from directions given in chapter 7.

Shade with good eating

If you are looking for a vine to give shade and food, *Sechium edule* (chayote) combines both virtues. It can be either a rampant perennial cucurbit or grown in colder regions as an annual. Like other vines, this strong-growing plant needs support. You may enjoy its rapid growth next spring and the delicate vegetable in late summer.

It will produce many delicate squash-like pear-shaped vegetables that are highly prized by flower arrangers for their faint green hue, interesting shape and soft texture, and by gourmets for the delicate flavor. Chayote vines may be started from fruits used in arrangements which often begin to grow in the hospitable warmth of the house. When outdoor planting time comes plant it whole, at an angle, about halfway in the ground with the stem exposed.

Visual garden dictionary

If you need encouragement to learn plant names (these are functional as well as pleasant to know), flower shows are for you. The horticultural division is a veritable visual garden encyclopedia, where named varieties compete for blue ribbon honors.

Keep an eye open for shows that feature tuberous begonias and fuchsias along with other garden beauties like Transvaal daisies. Aside from the excitement of seeing perfect specimens grown by careful gardeners, you may learn some new kinds to brighten your own bit of earth. Artistic arrangements combine good gardening with an arranger's skill to create living art forms with a few well-chosen blooms. One of the genuine pleasures of gardening is exhibiting. Growing for showing is an exciting goal.

Sunshine and water

If annual plants in your garden are leggy and show lack of vigor, check on the amount of sun each plant gets, not just on the longest day of the year—the summer solstice—but over a period of time. If sunlight is found to be adequate, look into the moisture situation. Sometimes casual observation fails to tell if it is too much or not enough. Reach a definite conclusion by probing the soil with a spading fork, shovel or a soil auger (see chapter 7).

Get ready for sweet pea planting. In heavy soil make a planter bed above ground. If you are tired of conventional long rows of sweet peas, experiment with unusual ways to grow these fragrant winter bloomers. Round beds supported by wire and planted to solid colors are resplendent.

A technique of enjoying sweet peas is not to plant so many that all the fun is taken away by the time consumed in clipping fading blossoms. Plant dwarf kinds in pots and window boxes in full sun for color and fragrance.

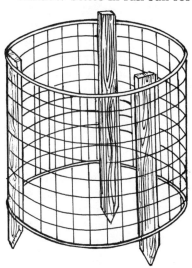

Easy-to-build sweet pea trellis, from 4-inch builders' wire. This frame is sturdy enough to double as compost bin. (See Chapter 7.)

The garden geranium will give almost year-round color. If these willing plants are grown in pots they may be moved about for best performance into full sun (indoors for winter), half sun as the days' warmth increases in spring, and almost complete but light shade now. Don't overwater, but use a mild stimulating liquid plant food like fish emulsion to maintain free flowering. Use a garden dust at least once a week to control small worms that eat the flower buds.

Discard the transients

Discarding annuals, whether flower or vegetable, before the last bloom has faded or the last bean picked is particularly difficult, but if we hold too long onto those transient plants, thrips, mildew and rust so disfigure foliage and flower that we may say, "I'm through with annuals." However, they are as essentially summer as the returning song birds. The trick is to plant those that are relatively pest free, have a long season and demand minimum grooming.

This upheaval leaves the garden bone-bare, unless you can move a few clumps of perennials to fill the vacuum. This is where plants in pots can come to the rescue. *Aster frikartii* responds to this treatment and can be depended upon to brighten an area with mauve-blue color through the rest of summer. It is my choice of the perennial asters—it requires no staking, is almost pest free, and is quite hardy. Look for new-to-you perennials in cans at nurseries and garden shops. Field-grown *gerberas* (Transvaal daisies) and other perennials may be bought balled in sacking, often in bloom, which takes the guesswork out of colors. Plant *gerbera* crowns slightly above the soil line for the perfect drainage they demand.

Is a new lawn on your must-have list?

This is also a good time to work up soil for a new lawn. Spread the area with a four-inch dressing of manure and one pound of calcium per square foot of soil, water to bring up weeds, hoe over or rototill and let the soil lay rough until early autumn planting. Investigate modern chemicals for soil fumigation and pre-emergence weed control. Some fumigants improve soil health by controlling harmful diseases and root insects as well as numerous weeds. The local farm adviser has the answers to this and numerous other garden problems.

Holes for subtropical trees to plant in early August should be partially dug and the loosened soil blended with manure and agricultural gypsum to overcome alkalinity or lime to correct acidity and to aid in mellowing the soil; keep moist.

Consider the best time for absence

It seems all the garden needs water at once, so it may not be a favorable time for an extended vacation. An early vacation avoids more than over-peopled accommodations. It avoids coming home to plants long in need of thorough soaking, clipping, feeding and staking and gives one a headstart with the autumn garden.

Watering the garden can be a delight or a most onerous chore. It hinges on one's WQ (water quotient.) Consider the areas of the garden to be watered, and the cost of each turn of the meter; weigh this against the price of equipment to distribute water efficiently. Take a walk around almost any neighborhood to see the devices other people use. Observe techniques of using sprinklers. Use a portable minute timer to gauge water sets. This gentle reminder will not replace sophisticated automatic regulators but may prevent either under- or over-watering. Finally, try to water when the air is quiet, as in early day, and set the sprinklers to carry water onto plants and not the sidewalk and on down the drain.

Work for pleasurable effects

Soil, food, water, plants and a flair for combining them add up to a pleasant garden. Mismatch any of these elements and you may have either a hodgepodge or an overgrown patch of plants falling over each other. Each season is known by the work that predominates. Winter is the big bareroot planting time, autumn traditional harvest, but summer brings a potpourri of chores.

Gardening reverses the adage "what goes up must come down," because we must plant before things can grow. Keep up with, or better yet, anticipate the season ahead by careful planning, and thorough soil renovation between crops, but take time to enjoy the beauty of the flowering earth.

A proud young farmer admires his autumn cabbages.

Chapter 3
Autumn

"Autumn is a weathercock
blows every way."
                    Christina G. Rossetti

September

This is the turning month—a turnabout in living routine and in gardening when the first breath of autumn sends a mild chill down summer's spine.

The pendulum of time has measured out three-fourths of the year, and brought the beginning of a new garden season. The autumnal equinox is not only a time of hurricanes, but marks a change in the gardener's almanac—day and night are of equal length. As the sun continues its southern orbit, balmy temperatures cause short-day flowers to bloom and nuts to mature, as if they were waiting for that northern breath of air. "Keeping" squash and pumpkins color the fields and gardens, and it is a good time to be out-of-doors, to enjoy the change of atmosphere.

The keynote is harvest

No matter which area you live in, these important harvests are a late autumn delight. Butternut, acorn and green-rind hubbard squash and pumpkins will be ripe for Halloween. Harvest these when the vines begin to wither.

Store in an airy cool place. These hearty vegetables will be welcome on winter menus, along with apples and pears. It is interesting that fruits and vegetables that come to maturity during late autumn may be used without preservation, which saves on refrigeration, canning or freezing. Nature's own storehouse protects with thick moisture-proof rinds and sugar-filled deliciousness.

September planting is to winter and early spring gardens what early spring planting is to summer and autumn production. Rare and choice plants grown from seed and cuttings give that special quality which distinguishes one garden from others, that makes a landscape special. What we do and plant now determines the kind of autumn, late winter and early spring garden we will enjoy. It is a time both of contemplation and activity, a time of waiting for late harvest to be completed. If the garden is small and land use at its maximum, a lingering harvest will mean longer gaps in color and yield.

Choose good companions

Plant association has much to do with plant health. Even in a small garden world we can avoid undue exposure of plants to various kinds of fungi and insects by careful grouping. These are undesirable combinations: pyracantha and avocados, roses and snapdragon. By a little planning and forethought many poor plant combinations can be avoided. Do a little research into plants' inherent disease and insect tendencies, and how much spraying can be eliminated by careful planting, watering and even harvest. Avoid spreading mildew and rust by not working among beans or sweet peas when the vines are damp.

Leaf vegetables are hardy

Plan a vegetable picking garden. Adventure beyond lettuce to spinach and endive, which will remain sweet and tender through the cool months and add piquancy to the salad bowl. Colorful rhubarb chard will be a welcome greens addition to a picking garden. Try hybrid dandelion from Burpee. The young foliage is good for salad, and may be tied up to blanch as is sometimes done with escarole. As the leaves age and thicken, they will be a tasty addition to the greens pot.

Two very worthwhile legumes for autumn and into winter are peas—both edible pod and the shelling kinds—and a lesser grown bean, Fava or English broad bean. The Fava bean is a coarse vigorous-growing annual, with robust gray foliage and enormous pods that shell out from six to ten beans; they resemble limas in size but are midway between a fresh pea and a fresh lima in taste.

Keep up with the season

Replant vegetables frequently enough to enjoy continuous yield. One way is to plant two kinds at the same time. For instance, bush beans will just about complete bearing when pole beans begin to give their delicious pods. You may reverse the planting technique by planting bush kinds as the pole beans go out of bearing. Wax beans will be a pleasant color change and are more cold tolerant than green ones. Lettuce is another vegetable that will work in this way. Plant both leaf and heading kinds at once. The delicious crisp leaves will be finished about the time the heading kinds are coming to table.

Keep gardening exciting

Gardening is only as static as our ideas. If our growth keeps pace with garden design, new methods and plant varieties, it remains an exciting adventure. Evaluate the passing garden parade with complete honesty. Weigh sunburn and insect bites and being shackled to a water and spray program against overflowing food lockers, colorful summer bouquets, fun days and evenings with family and neighbors.

"Yard-wide" may mean thirty-six inches to a seamstress and quite another thing to a gardener infatuated with bulbs scattered all over the place, blooming throughout the year. But if the "hosts of golden daffodils" effects are to be even approximated we need to begin planning now and compiling a list of bulbs and related flowers.

An old rule of thumb, "plant three times as deep as the bulb," like many other old theories, won't hold up in practice. Fist-size amaryllis, for instance, are set with their necks at soil level. Set anemone and ranunculus two inches deep; daffodils and their kin, four to six inches deep. If light shade is available, try a few hybrid lilies, and with the exception of Madonna (two inches deep), set these in open ground to eight inches, or midway in a six-inch pot.

Diminutive grape hyacinths may open the color display and be joined by a sextet of carpet flowers of delicate structure and hue. *Cerastium tomentosum* simulates a carpet of snow in full sun, but for a similar effect with cottage tulips that prefer light shade, perennial candy tuft will be better. Tulipmania may take the form of frustration in warm winter areas, but try planting Darwins eight inches deep in half shade after the soil has been cooled by a generous rain. Cottage tulips may be better growth insurance.

The end of summer

This month probably brings the end of the devastatingly hot weather. The only inhabitants around us that simply reveled in the summer-long heat were the vegetables: beans, cucumbers, summer squash, eggplant, peppers and corn. Some of these are now filling the shelves of our freezer, and as we enjoy their deliciousness before the open fires this winter, we will recall the warmth that brought them to perfection.

Autumn in many localities is a brief season that allows little leisure between the strenuous activity of summer and the slightly less demanding winter work program. This is the time for gathering in all our treasures—flowers for winter bouquets, bright gourds and other seed pods for arrangements. Bunches of spicy herbs hanging or spreading on trays to dry will now be put into containers to preserve their delicate aroma and taste.

How appropriate the term *fall* of the year, because much of our wealth of the season does just that. An important phase of autumn activity is knowing how and when to harvest almonds, walnuts and other nuts. As the outer husk begins to break, the nuts fall to the ground. Almost daily gleaning in late afternoon will keep rodents and ants from making inroads into the harvest we've been so anxiously awaiting.

It is also a time of promise for the bountiful garden of next year. Seed time and harvest come upon each other in the

A rustic herb garden makes a delightful focal point in the country garden of Mrs. Elizabeth Stone.

cultivated garden much as they do in wild nature, when harvest time is seed time. Exploding pods and silken parachutes carry seed of another year's bounty and beauty to new seed beds and fields.

Autumn chores

Early autumn is an auspicious time to overhaul the spray equipment for cleanup and dormant spray jobs that are upcoming.

Keep gopher traps working. Watch for tell-tale finely pulverized mounds of soil. Probe the area with a spading fork to locate main runways. A crushed leaf placed at the entrance after traps are set acts as enticing bait. Anchor traps to stakes with wire or light chain to prevent poaching cats carrying them away with the freshly caught game.

To free the soil of salts deposits left by the long months of summer irrigation, leach by generous sprinkler-watering (avoid flooding) as a prelude to autumn renovation. Dig the earth deeply, use a spading fork, then incorporate humus and dress with agricultural gypsum (in the western part of the country) or lime (in the eastern portion). Hoe into the top four inches or so, and rake smooth. Water again, lightly if the days are excessively warm and dry. Replant as soon as moisture and season are right.

Easy soil preparation

Sometimes a little common sense and planning will do more to take drudgery out of gardening than the fanciest machines. Spading when done in old country style is beyond the strength of most women and many men, but I have an effective method anyone can work. It consists of these simple steps: first, put on shoes with firm soles to protect your feet. Then begin by removing a spading forkful of soil. Set it to one side. Now push the spading fork as far into the soil as it will go, pull the handle backward until the soil cracks on the fork, then thrust the fork handle forward to arm's length. The loosened soil will fall into the space where the soil was removed.

As the work progresses it may be necessary to remove other forkfuls of dirt to keep an area for the loosened soil to fall into. The soil is not turned, because to do so would bring up raw dirt and put the fine humus underneath. This method effectively aerates the soil, breaks up compaction resulting from continuous irrigation and conserves the expensive humus mulch on top. Try it; you will agree!

Autumn gaiety

Chrysanthemums, autumn crocus and late dahlias unfurl multicolored banners. Only good gardening will assure prize-winning blooms for autumn flower shows of county fairs and flower societies scheduled when dahlias and chrysanthemums are at their best. Grooming flowers for showing is high adventure and a practical school for careful gardening.

Shift entire clumps of chrysanthemums to allow free air circulation to control rust and to extend color over more of the garden. Use those clumps to fill gaps left by maturing annuals.

Tuberous begonias announce their time of rest by diminishing growth. Those growing in the ground may be lifted with a shovel of the humusy soil and set in a dry place to ripen. Pots and baskets may be turned on the side (to ripen) in like manner. In any event, protect all ripening roots, bulbs and tubers from field mice.

Plan ahead

While the garden is getting this fresh start due to cooler nights, make plans for next year's garden, but keep the present plants attractive by staking, clipping fading flowers and giving quick-acting plant foods. Feed chrysanthemums with liquid manure for rapid growth (find directions in chapter 7). Scatter super-phosphate over deciduous bulb plantings. Use low-nitrogen plant food on shrub, tree and vine areas to sustain vigor rather than stimulate new growth.

Gardeners are of necessity long-range planners, but if plans are not put into action they go from one season to another without the reward and pleasure gardens can give. "Spring planting" in the fall is good gardening. Nurseries are exciting shopping centers these days for bulbs, new perennials and also for remainders of the season.

Good buys may not be bargains

Good buys can often be found in deciduous plants in five-gallon cans. Learn to judge quality and form—the amount of seasonal growth a plant has made and how it has been shaped during the summer. Don't be misled into thinking that because a plant has made a season's growth it is necessarily a better buy than a bareroot, dormant plant you might get in a few months.

When buying nursery plants, check the conditions where they are growing. Lath shelter and close-massed groupings provide special conditions that prevent evaporation from foliage. It may be wise to harden plants at home for a week or two in light shade, spaced apart, before setting them out in the garden. It is easier to sprinkle the foliage of a group of plants than to scamper about the garden to render first aid.

Transition is the name of the garden game. Each season sees about the same activity in the annual garden. Spring and autumn are big planting and unplanting times of the year. Take out aging plants, and renovate the soil with humus and plant food to nourish the crops that are to follow. Experiment with annuals, both flower and vegetable, you have not grown.

Say "farewell" to tired annuals

When summer-weary annuals begin to mildew and set seed despite our best efforts, it is well to have enjoyed the brilliant exuberance for a few weeks, but don't hold onto them after the fullness of bloom is past. Replace them with snaps, stock, primula, virginian stock (from seed) and other favorite short-day blooming annuals for late/early spring display. Set out new bulbs and nosegay plants for a colorful garden next spring.

Plants to make your garden gay after the annuals depart are plentiful. They range from dwarf perennial asters to the tallest autumn-flowering plants. The tree *Dahlia maxonii excelsea*, like the poinsettia in structure and culture, is seen to best advantage at the back of a shrub border. Now is a good time to search for it in gardens, and barter for stem cuttings when it is cut down in late winter. It, like many another handsome plant, has been pushed out of the mainstream of available plants by newer, although perhaps no more desirable, specimens.

Look for good companions

Snapdragon and calendula pair off well. Stock, larkspur, cornflower and annual phlox brighten areas of full sun. Primulas, cinerarias, lobelia, and forget-me-not prefer some shade. Free-flowering perennials that provide abundant color in the garden and for cutting include columbine, English daisy, coreopsis, gaillardia, Iceland poppy, penstemon and coral-bells. Most bulbs team up well with herbaceous plants. The combination does much to avoid the spent look that straight plantings of deciduous bulbs are famous for.

Rainbows packaged in tiny seeds await favorable conditions of soil and moisture to burst forth with new life to charm us with myriad colors. Hybridizers work zealously and persistently toward their ultimate goal: higher producing and more colorful plants. Almost any month some of these rainbows may be planted in your garden. Now is a favorable time. Not since March have we had weather conditions so conducive to seed germination.

Prepare for late roses

Prune and feed roses lightly for late bloom. Prune boxwood and privet hedges to allow time for new growth to harden up before frost. Do remedial pruning on deciduous trees while enough foliage remains to guide branch removal and thinning of small boughs that carry the leaf canopy.

Rewarding early morning rounds

Early morning hand picking of snails is often more rewarding than putting out bait, although this is additional assurance of control when you may not be able to patrol the garden. Following irrigation, particularly early in the day, many snails may be dislodged from tree trunks and dispatched with a leaf rake. Improvise various means to keep large leaves off the ground, which are incubating and hiding places for slugs, snails and sowbugs. Three-inch clay flower pots, turned on the side and faced away from the sprinklers, will protect the lethal element of bait against too much moisture.

Not only plants complete their growth cycle now; fungi spores are maturing, insects are beginning to go into winter attitudes, and some kinds of scale have reached adulthood. For a complete clean-up use a fungicide, insecticide and oil emulsion, but first wash down the plants. Spray is more effective on clean foliage. Follow directions on the containers implicitly. A complete spray used now will assure a cleaner garden next year (see chapter 6).

Welcome rains

Autumn rains generally bring another crop of weeds. Control by sprays is not as timely as prevention with pre-emergence chemicals, but be warned: most weed herbicides are not for areas being seeded, like lawns when a "specific" for crabgrass is used. Modern chemicals are useful tools or deadly enemies of plants, people and wildlife. Be sure *before* rather than sorry *afterward* (see chapter 7).

Check your watering

With an easy-to-make rain gauge a record of seasonal rainfall can be kept. The value of knowing how much rain falls in a year or season should not end there; relate it to soil moisture and plant growth to learn if supplemental water is needed or if soil is becoming waterlogged and plants drowned.

It may be easier to add additional water than to get rid of too much. Check the soil with a spading fork to determine if drainage problems are acute and do something about it. If basins that were made to facilitate summer watering of trees or shrubs remain filled for more than twenty-four hours, cut those berms with a shovel and divert excess water away from plants' roots. Fill low places where water stands with soil to the level of the surrounding areas. Move containers from under the drip of eaves.

Here are a few do's and don'ts for early autumn planning and planting. Do keep up insect control, moisture supply and food requirements. Summer insects and diseases thrive in hot and dry weather. Early morning hosing down of the garden creates humidity that is unfavorable to most mites and helps control mildew and rust. Don't water so late in the day that foliage cannot dry off before nightfall.

Do renew spent humus and basic plant food when renovating soil. Mulch camellias with old barnyard manure. Pay special attention to harvest of flowers, fruits, nuts and vegetables to ensure maximum yield and gourmet quality.

Olive bottle rain gauge

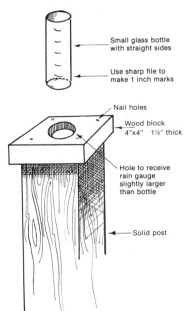

Small glass bottle with straight sides

Use sharp file to make 1 inch marks

Nail holes

Wood block 4"x4" 1½" thick

Hole to receive rain gauge slightly larger than bottle

Solid post

With this easily made rain gauge, you don't need to depend on the weather report to know how much water has come to your garden. Areas differ, sometimes even within a few miles.

October

Sun is the wine of life, never savored as in autumn, the true harvest season when one may determine the kind of vintage year it has been and balance the year's garden accounts. Debits will be conspicuous, but with courage and honest endeavor credits should predominate.

Enjoyment is a part of every harvest season, and may be particularly keen in autumn, but harvest, like seed time, can come almost any month by careful planning in mild climate regions. If you don't have a new harvest approaching you may as well live where winter is king.

Many weeks of fine autumnal-spring weather remain. Shorter days and cool nights bring fine growing weather. Keep up soil moisture and nutritional needs of winter-blooming annuals, and don't neglect the shrubs that brighten the landscape during winter. Be stingy with nitrogen; a 2–4–6 or similar formula will be best for now.

While garden chores fill the pleasant autumnal spring days, the emphasis shifts from a busy schedule of watering, controlling pests and constant clipping of fading flowers to soil preparation for planting.

To get a headstart on autumn remove spent flowers and vegetables, work the soil deeply, add manure, agricultural gypsum or lime, water thoroughly by sprinkling, let mellow, rake smooth and replant for fall, winter and spring.

Autumn fruit drop, particularly of persimmons, is to be expected. The tree may cast off much of the crop. Circling the branches with a knife, just through the bark (no bark is removed as in girdling) may slow the sap-flow for a day or two, and halt the fall of the fruit. It's worth a try. Experiment on nonfruiting branches to develop the technique.

Stretch your harvest season

Turn bushel baskets or cartons over eggplant and pepper plants and heap soil over their roots to prevent frost damage. Also, tie three strong stakes together and drape nightly with canvas to form a tepee over bean and tomato plants. These are a few ideas to lengthen the harvest and postpone inroads on the bounty of the pantry shelf, freezer and root cellar.

To further prolong the natural food supply, pull tomato vines before frost. Hang them in a garage or other sheltered place and tomatoes will continue to ripen.

Save for feathered friends

Here is a different kind of harvest that will provide interesting winter entertainment. Tie into smallish bundles any and all annual and perennial seed stalks and seed heads for winter birds. You may tie up a fresh bundle as they thrash out the seeds, and especially after snow or rain provide fresh food for these live pest-control agents that are always on the job. Most regions have small seed-eaters, varying from area to area like other of nature's creatures. Chickadees, warblers, and creepers are birds of dooryards as well as forest, meadow and garden.

Get rid of winter boarders

An application of a three-way fall clean-up spray that contains fungicide, insecticide and oil emulsion aims to destroy eggs and spores of various summer insects, diseases and scale, and is good insurance for a cleaner, thriftier garden next year (see chapter 6). Wet the ground beneath the plants. Rake up and dispose of fallen fruit that may harbor disease spores. Sanitation in the garden is a good means of prevention. Use whitewash or latex paint to reflect the slanting winter sun which shines directly against deciduous tree trunks and causes sunburn.

Inviting tender leaves of annuals are a banquet for chewing and sucking insects unless sharp control is carefully exercised. Inspect insecticide shelves of local markets. Only an informed gardener can take full advantage of the products modern science is developing, and only an informed gardener can be sure he is getting the correct formula for his condition. Read the *caution* paragraph carefully, particularly on aerosol cans, for ant control to find out if it is safe to use on foliage. Don't neglect the ever-present easy-to-use water power, either as a strong force of water with a nozzle, or as a hose-attached spray device, to dispense insecticides. If vegetables are a part of your garden, nonpoisonous sprays assume added importance—rotenone, pyrethrines and Blackleaf 40 are three of these.

Blessed autumn rains

The first rains of autumn are often delayed, so take care to ensure even moisture over the garden. I use a sprinkler that sprays softly, but wide, for overall watering, and a narrower one for drenching trees and shrubs that need deeper moisture than garden plants.

The cycle of the seasons gives time to pause, to reflect on other seasons' triumphs and to try to remedy mistakes. One common neglect is lack of thorough soil preparation between plantings. Feeding and soil renovation are an autumn must. Enzyme-rich barnyard manure provides food and humus and is good soil tonic.

Fruitful shade trees

Explore the landscape value of various nut-bearing plants. While most are deciduous, macadamia from the Pacific islands is a medium-size tree with handsome, prickle-edged, leathery, evergreen leaves. New hybrids have softer, easier to crack shells. They are hardier against frost than other subtropicals. Pecan and/or walnut trees make impressive shade trees in a few years, and yield quantities of nutritious nuts. Filbert (hazel nut) bushes develop into interesting deciduous hedges, with early spring, long catkins. Choose correct kinds for cross-pollination to ensure bountiful crops of the delicious, always expensive nuts.

Bulbs to brighten the garden

Besides those bulbs already mentioned, here are a few that can go in now and be ready to bloom in spring. Woodland bluebells (*Scilla*) and delicate *Ornithogalum umbellatum, Leucojum vernum, Nerine, Lycoris, Sprekelia* and *Babiana* (will provide for a bluest blue); and white or pink dainty *Zephyranthes* will brighten a border edge with periodic bloom and evergreen reed-like foliage. Many of these will be in stores soon. Others will come in through autumn and spring months. Like vegetables and fruits, easy-to-grow desirable flowers have their season, too.

The big bulb-planting season is a time of decision. Lessen next spring's chore of clearing away maturing leaves and spent flower stalks by giving careful consideration to the kind and number of bulbs planted, as well as their location. Decide whether to continue to grow all deciduous bulbs or to plant more of those with evergreen foliage.

Here's a safe way to lift bulbs. Plant large kinds individually in small wire baskets; diminutive ones may be double or even triple planted. The soil/root mass can then be lifted as bloom fades without interfering with the bulbs' maturity.

No such simple harvest device will work with large clumps of dahlia roots, but they may be hastened toward maturity without lessening the vigor of the tubers for next year. With either a shovel or spade, cut around the roots, ten to fifteen inches from the center stems, to shovel depth. Cut straight down, to avoid root injury, but at the same time give a slight lifting motion to break the tap roots. Cut the spent flower stalks down to eight or ten inches and allow the soil to become dry. The tubers should be ripe around Thanksgiving. Unharvested tubers may rot in wet winter soil. In any event, aside from economy, the bed is free for other crops and will certainly result in finer quality blooms next season. Add to these advantages the joy of increase and control of root insects and diseases. The soil where they have been growing will need food and humus for the next crop.

As with other garden chores, there is more than one theory. I prefer the one that says "divide as soon as dug," when the eyes will be visible and the blind ones may be discarded. Label and store in sand or other media to prevent excessive drying in a cool place.

Prevention of next season's thrips

Clean glad corms before they are stored or replanted. Save the cormlets; many will flower after the first growing season in the garden. The flower spikes may not be as large, but these are not baby glads; they belong to an entirely different race. Bulb specialists offer true baby glads. Because of early blooming they are not as subject to thrips damage as are hybrids, and are more in scale with average-size homes than the giant florist types. They are offered by some growers as miniatures.

Detail of Gladiolus corm. Cormels—small bulbs—form at base of new corm. Use an old tablespoon to separate the corms.

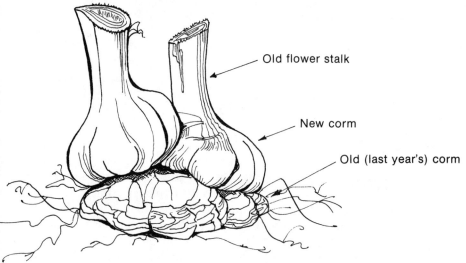

Old flower stalk

New corm

Old (last year's) corm

The much-neglected watsonias, with much the same growth habits as glads, should be dug at least in alternate years. However, since it is difficult to remember which year it was done, I like to lift them each year. The white ones are elegant in light shade, and the salmon tones blend with certain geraniums and petunias, as do the soft lavender. Where tall bulb flowers are wanted, try watsonias.

Indian summer

Autumn planting has the advantage of warm soil, cooler nights and lovely Indian summer days, when to be working out-of-doors is pure delight. Weigh the present price for established plants (perhaps twice that of bareroots) with the advantage of pleasant planting weather, against less expensive bareroot planting in January or February, when soil may be wet and sticky and the weather cold.

Things to check off and be aware of at either planting time to obtain quality are: good branching form for the species, signs of seasonal growth, roots not growing out of drainage holes in cans, absence of unhealed scars which may become areas for insect breeding and/or the beginning of rot.

Don't try to squeeze the last reward from plants; keep new ones coming. This continuous gardening can be most easily accomplished by establishing small plants in four-inch plant bands set in flats or frames, or in three- or four-inch clay pots heeled in sand to prevent drying out, or by spacing wider apart in flats, say four-by-four-inch squares rather than the usual two-by-two-inch spacing. Growing-on and the suggestions that follow will be easier in a nursery situation. Many plants can be grown under a shelter no larger than ten feet square. This can be a lath shelter or shade of a tree.

Every gardener loves bargains

At this time of year nurseries put plants growing in gallon cans on sale. This may be done to stimulate business and get rid of slow movers, but mainly to avoid shifting stock into larger cans and to clear out pot-bound stock. Those that are not too root-bound may be rehabilitated; don't consider them as bargains, however, but as a challenge. It takes skill and patience to bring such plants back to normal health.

Repotting tips: examine the roots, and cut in several places those that are growing in circles. This encourages a normal root system. Shifting plants from one-gallon size cans to fives gives ample root space for renewed growth. Keeping them in a home nursery like this allows closer observation and a better chance for survival than if they are planted out in the open ground.

Other advantages of a small home growing-on nursery are to provide a resting area where perennials that need dividing may be heeled-in until spring propagation time comes, to free the space in the border for quick-to-bloom annuals and bulbs, but best of all to allow thorough soil renovation, which is usually undertaken at this time of year. We are constantly on the lookout for ways to lessen this arduous job and if the garden areas are designed with the use of mechanical devices like rototillers in mind, this is one way to overcome so much back-breaking, time-consuming toil.

Render first aid to weary lawns and ground covers

After months of summer watering most lawns need some renovating. If water stands after short watering, spiking the ground should open hardpan created by a constant-level water table. If a mechanical device can be borrowed or rented, fine, but it can be done with a spading fork. Where a considerable area is involved you may think the task interminable, but a square yard done each day will eventually end the job. Then feed and reseed with a winter-hardy grass. Fescues for partial shade or perennial rye are worth trying.

It is a good time to mow the strawberry ground cover, but set the mower blades high enough to avoid damage to plant crowns. Mowing is more effective if long loose stems are raised with a rake before mowing. After excess foliage has been removed, look for ants mounding soil in plant crowns—a warning that root aphids, scale or ground mealybug are present. Using the dilution for spraying, mix a quantity of an insecticide and oil emulsion spray and pour about one-half cupful into the crown of each plant. The soil should be moist at time of application. Much the same mowing technique can be used to refurbish a Bermuda grass lawn.

While in the renovating mood, get out the spray gun,

pruning shears and saw, rake and mower—it's time to do over the garden once again. But don't be overawed by this prodigious workload; consider one job at a time.

Refurbish garden tools

We cannot lay down the shovel and hoe in a year-round garden climate, but with slackening garden work we may refurbish them. Sand and oil wooden handles, tighten or replace loose or broken handles, sharpen to a fine cutting edge tools that have become dulled by long and continuous use, and in other ways put the tool locker in order.

Tools kept under cover when not in use will not only last longer but stay in better condition. Gloves will protect hands against prickles, thorns and dust, and infection by poisonous plants. Use leather gloves for dusty and thorny work and some sort of weatherproof ones for wet jobs and transplanting seedlings. We may thoroughly enjoy the feel of soil in our bare hands, but we need to be able to do more delicate work, so use gloves and keep happy.

Leaf-falling time of year

Autumn is the golden season of the year. In Indian folklore October is the leaf-falling month. Instead of burning these mineral-rich treasures or carting them off with other rubbish, compost them (see chapter 7 and The Orbit).

We are but little past the autumnal equinox—September 23—which the calendar marks as the true beginning of autumn, and already the ever-widening gap between the length of day and night brings to perfection short-day blooming plants. Chrysanthemum and perennial asters are highlights; the pastel tones of autumn asters pleasingly complement the warm colors of chrysanthemums. By careful selection it is possible to have some of these in bloom up to Thanksgiving.

Buy garden-type chrysanthemum plants now. These leftovers may not look very promising, but if the root is healthy you will be ahead by getting them and planting in an out-of-the-way place until next spring when slips may be made of the new growth.

Prepare for approaching frost

If killing frost frequents your area, provide protection for tender plants like geraniums, pelargoniums and fuchsias (see chapter 6). These will continue to bloom through winter in a sunny window.

Listen to the fruit-frost weather reports, use common sense based on previous experience and cover tender plants. Delay pruning tender and even half-hardy plants until spring. Foliage helps prevent frost damage to wood structure. New growth that might come as a result of pruning will be more subject to frost damage.

Assorted sizes of paper cartons are excellent shelter against frosty nights. They do not need tying, will not allow frost to scorch the foliage, and can be picked up so the sun can warm plants and soil during the day (see chapter 6).

There are often two extremes to winter: high (cold) moisture that drops temperatures to the danger point, and dryness (below normal rainfall) with high temperatures that favors growth of tender-to-frost plants.

Pruning of deciduous plants can be undertaken in earnest when most of the leaves are off them and you can look through the tree's branch structure and find out what went amiss while the tree was modestly clothed in summer greenery.

Invigorating work for cooler days

Noticeably shorter days, cooler nights and invigorating air make good weather for changes in the landscape, as soon as rain comes. Renovate beds with manure and agricultural gypsum as plants are removed. Begin making holes for bareroot roses, shrubs and trees: blend adobe soil or clay with manure and gypsum for planting rather than using imported soil that may give only temporary root growth (see chapter 7).

Plan for good color

While some garden beds are empty, begin to plan and to plant a border. With the long growing season in mild climates, plants last only a few years at best, so we don't go in for complete soil building that English or even eastern gardeners do. But whether it is a bed of annuals or a perennial border, any plant grouping needs a carefully made plan to be a success. Begin by making a list of flowers to bloom during each season or at a particular time when you may wish the garden to be at its best.

Here are a few perennials I give an A on performance, appearance, ease of growth and beauty: *Aster frikartii,* heliotrope, *gerbera* daisy, *Alstroemaria* and bulb-like flowers with evergreen foliage. An ideal is to have as much evergreen material as possible, and to have each plant be in harmony with its neighbors.

Best buys may be found in containers

Shop for best buys in deciduous plants in containers and for field-grown living evergreens for Christmas trees. Planting techniques for those either balled in burlap or in containers begin with digging adequate holes (see section on planting in chapter 6).

Divide clumps of agapanthus, daylily and other summer-flowering bulbs, roots and perennials. It is too near bloom-time to work over clivia and other winter-flowering bulbs. Use this rule of thumb: reset, prune or plant following bloom, not before. Disbud camellia japonica and look for Sasanqua camellias that may be showing color. Choose carefully for growth habits to fit the area you have to fill.

We cease being amateur gardeners when our failures can be analyzed, looked at objectively and prevented from occurring again. But no matter our age in years, we are always young as gardeners. The challenges of ever-changing seeds, plant foods, soil amendments and spray materials keep gardeners continually alert. An advantage of a home garden is that expensive foods and elegant flowers for house and garden adornment cost little more to grow than ordinary ones.

Protect your plants from birds

Returning white-crown sparrows may think their cheerful song a fair exchange for tender lettuce and garden pea foliage. When these are eaten they may vary their diet with broccoli, ranunculus and anemone leaves. Ingenuity is needed to thwart the sparrows, brown tohees and other ground-feeding birds.

These preventive measures have worked wonders while the plants are hardening up: inverted plastic berry boxes cover very small plants; large individual plant covers may be fashioned of nylon screen wire which give more room; but for larger plants and row crops, improvise quonset-shaped wires and drape with nylon screening. Plenty of sun comes through the net, but the birds will need to look elsewhere for their salad.

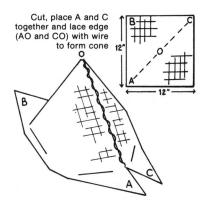

Cut, place A and C together and lace edge (AO and CO) with wire to form cone

When young plants outgrow the protection afforded by plastic berry boxes, this plant cap made from screen wire will do the work until they outgrow the need.

You may cater to these delightful live pest-control agents with a row of unprotected lettuce just for them, in return for the aphids they eat. Ranunculus is one of their special favorite "greens." Plant these small roots in flats or shallow boxes, space them about three inches apart, and cover the box with netting. This method has an advantage of conserving space and allows later planting, but requires more careful tending than open-ground planting.

Cooling late daytime pleasant

Cooling late daytime is ideal for strenuous garden projects, some of which you may not have been able to tackle during the busy summer along with vacation and other activities of the season. With the ever-shortening days we lose the pleasant after-work hour for gardening. Halloween brings the assurance that fall is really here.

November

November brings our traditional holiday; make it truly Thanksgiving. From this happy festival until Christmas the bustling activity seldom relaxes, so it is fortunate that garden jobs are not too pressing. However, do not neglect the annual clean-up chores—uprooting old plants, dormant spraying and preparation for planting bareroot plants.

If autumn is dry, water

Watering must continue if a bountiful rain has not come. A good water slogan is "adequate but not excessive." Add to the natural rainfall to make up the shortage and to meet the needs of plants. Serious damage results to even dormant plants if soil becomes too dry to supply moisture to plant tissue.

While this is a holiday season for us, our gardens do not observe holidays. Theirs is a year-long time of growing, ours a year-long time of tending them and enjoying the increase. Each season has its rewards. November is lavish with burnished colors, and while the lands are still lit with an autumn blaze of goldenrod, begin to look elsewhere for color. Trees and shrubs that bear colorful fruit during winter will be enjoyed by wild things, too. When cutting sprays of berries, avoid die-back by cutting to lateral branches. Do not leave stubs!

Set up a scorecard for deciduous trees

Now is a good time to judge the garden in terms of required shade, and of equal importance, winter sun. A large-growing deciduous tree will do double duty. A scorecard for judging deciduous trees should take into consideration the time of spring leafing and autumn leaf drop. Those that retain their leaves through early winter, dribbling a few each day, not only defeat the purpose of a deciduous tree, but create a prolonged clean-up job.

A plus score for sweet gum (liquidambar) is one of diversified autumn tones, but it falls into the leaf-dribbling class. On the other hand, *Ginkgo biloba* and Chinese pistache give high color and quick leaf drop, which lessens leaf raking and will admit welcome autumn and winter sun. A tree that is a very early leafer deprives us of late winter/early spring sun, and where late frosts sometimes occur the first flush of green may be nipped, which sets the tree back considerably. Deciduous trees that flower before the leaves appear are numerous. The trick here is to choose flower and leaf color for landscape harmony and beauty. This is an advantage in choosing sweet gum when in autumn leaf, since the colors vary from old rose to reds and yellows.

Shop early for living Christmas trees

If you are planning to grow a living Christmas tree, begin shopping soon. Field-grown conifers should be in nurseries this month and are generally superior to container-grown plants. Select a tree to fit your climate, space and garden design and leave to parks and estate-size gardens the elegance of "Christmas-tree lanes" of deodar cedars or other conifers.

Develop good planting techniques

Developing good planting techniques is important now that we will be setting out plants from containers and those balled in burlap. A word about planting: always remove plants from tin cans, but do not remove the sacking or canvas, as new roots will grow through it. It may be advisable and will be more tidy to cut away the cloth that remains above ground after planting.

Many plants are often unhappy where we plant them despite our best efforts to give them the recommended location. Soil drainage, exposure to sun, shade or wind may prevent growth. These are some of the reasons for moving plants from one place to another, but a more profitable one is to extend them to other areas. Autumn is an ideal time for this operation. The weather is fine, and we are in a cleaning-up frame of mind so this kind of gardening fits the season's mood.

We often see herbaceous perennials left for several years without lifting and dividing that have grown into great untidy masses of old leaves and stems which provide hiding and breeding places for scale, insects, slugs, snails, sowbugs and earwigs, and result in an ever-diminishing flower display.

Where herbaceous peonies thrive, it may be a good time to divide those and share or exchange with neighbors and friends. It is not necessary to use every precaution when moving most perennials, because these are often broken up, but it is necessary with shrubby plants. After a new location has been decided upon, make the new hole and mix enough soil to replant before lifting the old plant. Choose a fine day. Moving even medium-size plants calls for great care and brawn.

My transplanting formula

Here's my transplanting formula: to facilitate handling, bind the boughs into bundles by encircling them and tying with strong cord. Soak the soil around the shrub two or three days before moving day. Dig toward the plant; go all around the perimeter at the root ends with a spading fork. After the feeder roots are free, use a shovel to remove surplus dirt. Use these tools alternately. Some of the roots may need to be cut. Do this carefully to avoid injury and seal the larger cuts with Treeseal or a similar compound. Keep the plant in balance by pruning branches.

Just to dig carefully around the plant often isn't enough.

Wrapping (balling) the roots in burlap is insurance against losing soil from them. The technique is not difficult and consists of using two lengths of burlap or old canvas about a foot wide and a yard long, laid across each other to form a cross. Larger shrubs of course will need more yardage. Gently lift the plant onto the doubled cloth, bring the ends up and tie securely with strong cord about the plant stem. Then take the cord under the earth ball and lace four or five times around the roots. All of this makes moving plants easier and there is less likelihood of loss.

If we can forgo the urge to use our ever-present feet as tools for firming soil we can do a better job of planting. If we change *tramp* to *tamp* and employ a firm stick such as a discarded ball bat or a two-by-two-inch piece of wood of convenient length as a potting stick we will do a much better job of firming soil. For one thing, because of the wide-spread branches of some shrubs, it is not easy to get feet into the basin to tramp the soil firm, and it might also injure the roots.

Perhaps a timetable isn't enough

A timetable for garden chores may not get you to where you are going but should show what to aim for. Colorful nautical jargon like "batten down the hatches" and "shipshape," translated into garden know-how, connotes getting ready for foul weather. Cautious gardeners prepare for it; the indifferent ones lose valuable plants each winter.

So, check the stakes of plants, renew, loosen and otherwise make the lashings secure and comfortable. Loosening the tying devices of plants is necessary because the increase in the diameter of a tree's stem may not have been noticed during the busy time of watering and harvest. Stakes rot away, plants outgrow them and where ties are allowed to break and are not replaced, the plant may rub on the top of the stake and wear the bark away. This is particularly prevalent in tree roses. Tying devices need slackening off almost yearly, and should be renewed before they rot away. No. 14 weatherproof insulated wire makes a serviceable tie. It is pliable enough to twist, but does not unwind and is large enough to prevent damage to the bark of the plant. Further protection is afforded with a short length of old garden hose.

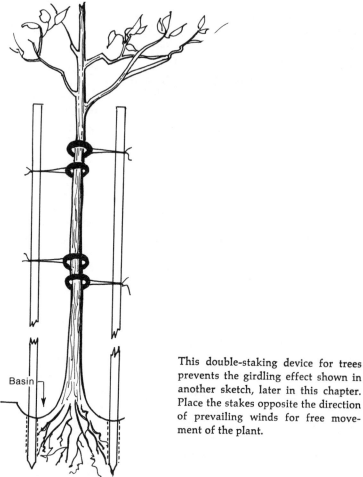

This double-staking device for trees prevents the girdling effect shown in another sketch, later in this chapter. Place the stakes opposite the direction of prevailing winds for free movement of the plant.

When tying a tree to its stake with wire, I place my hand into the loop that goes around the tree to ensure ample room for the tree to have gentle movement. Then I make three or four turns of the wire before passing it twice around the stake. In this way the tree is not tied tightly to the stake, which so often causes it to grow over the wire, girdling it, but it may move gently within this ample circle and so develop "backbone." Where plants are going to require staking for more than two years, it is better to use the double stake device shown here.

Expectant hopeful rain

As year's end approaches rain is more certain. Weather changes which often occur with the autumnal equinox may bring the first rain to catch us with uncompleted projects—open garden beds half-manured, seed boxes filled with soil but not planted, bulbs in brown paper bags unplanted.

We like to savor the luxury of rejuvenating moisture over the entire garden at once. This has not happened since the last spring rain when we resigned ourselves to the long dry summer and autumn and to becoming the dispenser of moisture ourselves.

If autumn rains are light, around an inch, supplement with a like amount of water, preferably by sprinkling. Better yet, when rain is forecast, break out the hoses and anticipate it. Rain falling on previously moistened soil will soak in better and do considerable soil leaching, and even a light rain will give deep penetration. Along with these notes about stretching water the sound of rain on the roof would be the most welcome autumn treat.

Autumn harvest

On a blustery November day an entire crop of deciduous tree leaves may be blown off and snuggle under, around and through almost every plant in the area. You may hear an irate neighbor scold, "Leaves go home!" There is no way to keep leaves where they grew, but in turn, you may find those of other gardens littering your shrubbery. It is a small price to have to pay for delicious summer fruit. This heavy leaf-fall coincides with National Garden Clean-up Week.

Not all are onions

You can grow a potpourri of *alliums*. Each will have a distinctive flavor for seasoning. Chives are the most delicate and will self-sow in unlikely places about the garden. Leek plants that were not harvested will likewise scatter seeds about. It is better practice not to let these ripen, but allow the old leek stalks to remain for a while so the bulb-like root offsets can form for continued crops. (But dig the old plants and divide the tubers and replant for a continuous supply of this elegant vegetable.)

Shallots may begin to grow again unless harvested when the tops turn brown in early autumn. Onions are too well known to need much comment, but for a continuous supply of fresh green ones, sow seed in spring and autumn. Cooking onions in various colors and flavors are easy to grow from "sets."

The onion family

Chive (*Allium schoenoprasum*) seems not at all burdened with its ponderous name and self-sows in odd corners. In late spring the heads of purple-lavender flowers create quite a show.

Garlic (*Allium sativum*) is next easiest to grow. In our garden if at least one clove breaks free when harvesting, next spring we have more garlic, whose properties of aphid control work wonders when growing along with broccoli.

Shallots (*Allium ascalonicum*) bear their cloves above the ground and are prolific producers, keep all winter and are delightful additions to dishes that might not be complemented with plain onions.

Leek (*Allium porrum*), the giant of the tribe, can be enjoyed much of the season, from delectable additions to soups and stews to its tall flower stalks, which will surprise you one day from the leeks you failed to eat soon enough. We let the flower heads mature (which are genuine conversation makers); when root offsets develop, we use them to keep the plants coming on, rather than go through the longer process of starting from seed.

Onion (*Allium cepa*), the best known and most universally used of the genus, is not all that common. They grow almost year-round as delectable tender green shoots, mature keeping kinds and as scallions.

Ropes of onion and shallots make individual choice easy, protect the roots from mildewing and add a colorful note to the garden room.

Winter is traditional pruning time. Ernest Schoefer, developer
of Mendocino Coast Botanical Garden tackles this
prodigious job with the right tool. Pruning techniques are
described in Chapter 6.

Chapter 4
Winter

"The winter nights against my window-pane
Nature with busy pencil draws designs
Of ferns and blossoms and fine spray of pines."
T. B. Aldrich

December

Winter is the end of the calendar year. The first day of winter precedes Christmas by only a few days, but all month we will be experiencing the coming of the year's shortest day. It is with good reason that American Indians call December the "long night moon," because winter comes officially this month. Evening fires, garden chores and festive preparations call upon our time, but we must also pause to enjoy the year's ending.

Take pride in your garden

Gardening is a many-splendored thing if we can have a glow of pride when the monthly returns are computed. It is necessary to consider the routine that brings the garden to fruition and resolve for better performance each season. One way to do this is with a garden journal, but devotion must be practiced in keeping it up. If most of the pages are blank at season's end, guideposts you found along the way this year will not help to bring about next year's successes.

Little leisure for gardeners

During winter days one expects a bit of leisure, so it may seem like the last straw to have to continue with such day-to-day chores as watering, controlling aphids on young annuals, baiting for sow and pill bugs, snails and slugs, and staking tall-growing plants. Regardless of your thermometer reading, chores that belong to winter are a part of garden making everywhere. The size and kind of garden you have will determine which, and to what extent each activity is carried out. Adapt them to your own garden, add to or deduct from them, but there is no shortcut in the basic winter routine if one wishes to ensure a more productive garden in the new season.

Consider these few chores: bareroot planting, balled in burlap or container-grown, is generally done when plants become available and weather permits. Prune last summer's side branches of wisteria to two buds; feed with a 5–10–5 formula now rather than next spring. Early feeding with a low-nitrogen fertilizer will not encourage leaf growth at the expense of flowers. Tidy up to avoid a crisscross tangle of branches.

Production and length of harvest of bush peas will be improved by a string framework. Drive stakes at the ends of short rows, or four to six feet apart in longer rows. Run strong cord along either side of the plants, and fasten the cord to all the stakes. If plants outgrow the first string retainer, add additional rows. Some support is necessary during storms to prevent plants being broken over with the weight of moisture. It is a good idea in any season for tidiness and ease of harvest as well as space conservation.

Small bamboo withes make wicket-type plant aids. Bend and stick both ends into the soil. Overlap them to form scallops in a continuous circle about helleborus, campanula, lettuce and any other plants that have leaves near the ground. Such a device will prevent rain-spattered foliage and snail and slug damage of lettuce. If bamboo is not available, stiff wire may be used.

Garden gifts that grow

Christmas is a time of giving and receiving; why not give your garden a gift this year? A prim Elizabethan herb garden planted about a sundial will be an interesting and useful motif. To keep this accent planting from becoming overgrown and weedy, choose plants that remain neat. Thyme, sweet marjoram and oregano will give pleasant leaf control.

Because sundials are usually located in full sun, plants shoud be drought-tolerant. Herbs that need half-shade, like the tasty salad herb, burnet, would not be suitable. Sage is too robust, but would be delightfully complementary if grown nearby in pots along with English lavender. A few pot marigolds (calendula) will add winter color. Viola (hearts' ease or Johnny jump-up) will add gaiety and charm.

Portable gardens are in high favor. Consider them for garden-minded friends. Remember, Christmas is almost only tomorrow.

Give yourself some "good taste"

Give yourself and your kitchen a delightful Christmas present with a collection of potted herbs. Choose kinds to fit your temperature and light. Even though herbs are easy to grow, they have their climate preferences. Most are perennial, but chives and most parsley will take a dormant rest and usually grow again, and are on the desirable snipping list.

No kiss for mistletoe

Doorways hung with mistletoe are a part of the gaiety and legend of Christmas. However, gardeners are not as concerned with the folklore and legend of mistletoe as the damage this destructive parasitic plant does to valuable shade trees and what to do about it.

No effective herbicide spray has been developed to control mistletoe because its specialized roots get the necessary moisture from the cambium layer of the host tree. A spray that would kill the parasite plant would seriously damage the tree. Early detection is easy in deciduous trees, but when it attacks evergreen oaks only an observant eye can discover it in the first stage of growth. When it occurs on small branches, cutting them off is the surest method of control. Where it has been growing for a long time on larger limbs, it may be necessary to remove considerable wood, and may require help from a tree surgeon.

Render first aid to your Christmas tree

Whether your tree is a cut or living tree, moisture is vital; it is perhaps easier to keep a tree moist that is planted in a container. Consider the needs of the growing tree first, and choose one in scale and character with your garden. The dwarf *Pinus mughus* adds an unusual evergreen note to the landscape, or the adaptable Aleppo pine, *Pinus halepensis*, may be used as an informal decorative tree and later trained as an oversized bonsai to accent a special garden scene.

Cut at least two inches from the base of a cut tree for better water absorption. If a commercial tree holder is not available, center the tree stem in a large pail and use bricks or stones to make it secure. Fill the pail with water and keep it filled. If tip-growth begins to wilt, clip it off. It is good to see that the popularity of cut trees is waning in favor of growing things, and that people are beginning to appreciate the tree as a center or a motif rather than a traditional pine or fir Christmas tree.

It takes faith to be a gardener

Some people see any season as a good year, knowing full well that the failures of one growth time may be eclipsed by the successes of the next. This may depend upon what manner of garden you are tending, and there are also ways to combat off seasons and to harness the weather, so to speak.

A nursery growing-on area and/or cold frame is plant growth insurance well worth the cost. Cold-region gardeners wouldn't even contemplate a garden without cold frames, and warm latitudes should come to know the advantages, too. In a mild climate the frame doesn't need to be placed as deeply in

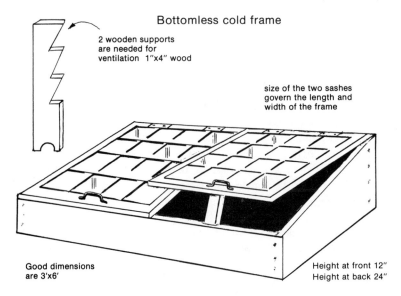

Bottomless cold frame

2 wooden supports
are needed for
ventilation 1"x4" wood

size of the two sashes
govern the length and
width of the frame

Good dimensions
are 3'x6'

Height at front 12"
Height at back 24"

You may make a simple cold frame from discarded window sash. Bottom heat may be provided with rather fresh horse manure, where more warmth is needed; in which case, remove about four inches of soil and fill with the manure. Cover with about two inches of soil. It is necessary to provide for ventilation. We like the notched member better than a plain stick. It is more secure and the amount of air may be regulated, rather than using a stick as shown. It is better to grow plants in pots and/or small seed boxes than directly in the soil.

the soil, because the frost line may not be more than two or three inches; in addition, since daytime temperatures are higher, bottom heat is seldom needed unless hardwood cuttings are to be rooted.

Perennial favorites

For length of production, few vegetables can compete with asparagus. A four-week crop with excellent freezing qualities recommends this always expensive gourmet food plant. Twelve roots will supply a family of two. To plant, dig a trench a foot wide and a foot deep. Form a ridge of soil about four inches high along the center, spread the fleshy roots a foot apart over this, and cover the crowns with two inches of soil. As new spring growth starts, begin covering with good soil to the level of the garden and mulch with manure. Water, either by sprinkler or in a furrow around the bed.

Deciduous trees give winter sunshine

Much can be said in favor of trees that drop their leaves in winter. Most important is that deciduous trees are cleaner, few lose as many leaves during summer as evergreen trees do, they are often a lusher green and many are generous bloomers. They are the plant world's crowning achievement. Besides these desirable traits, they may be bought bareroot while dormant for a fraction of what trees of comparable size cost in containers later in the year. When fruit is added to these other admirable attributes, we may discover the rainbow's end in these large landscape specimens.

Dormant spraying time

In getting ready to spray, decide upon the type of applicator, the spray material to use and when to do the work. Timing is not as important in dormant spraying as for insects or fungi, but is an essential phase of gardening (see chapter 6).

Spray all roses following dormant pruning and planting of new kinds. Use a dormant spray chemical. Examine plants for signs of new scale, and if these are present add an oil emulsion to the copper sulfate—Bordeaux spray (see chapter 6). Moisten the soil beneath plants with the spray for control of any enemies that may have fallen with the leaves. Concerned environmentalists will be glad to know that dormant spray chemicals are noninsidious. They ensure a cleaner, healthier garden next season by killing overwintering pests and their eggs (particularly spider mites and scale), fungus spores, peachleaf curl and brown rot of apricots. They will ensure plump disease-free cane berries and healthy roses.

Spray all dormant fruits now if this was not done in November, or you may delay this important phase of growing deciduous plants until new roses and other plants are in the garden. But it must be done in any event no later than January for effective control. Read the section in chapter 6 on insects and diseases for a thorough discussion.

Manure—the all-around soil amendment

When renovating soil between crops, consider the value of manure as a soil conditioner. It is the only humus with an appreciable amount of nitrogen. Most other humuses need added nitrogen to do the dual work of soil conditioning and feeding.

Feeding now will be confined to spreading manure over dormant plant beds. Delay until March the feeding of evergreen plants and applying a complete plant food to perennials, annuals and vegetables, except where signs of malnutrition are evident.

Fashion plays an important role in gardens, too. New plants are discovered, and old favorites hybridized almost beyond recognition. Even vegetables change identity and are in a fair way to compete with marigolds and zinnias for a place in the sun. Several million new vegetable gardens are begun each year to ensure chemical-free food and to reduce living costs. The ecology movement is not entirely responsible for the new interest in growing vegetables; budgets need slimming to keep within the food allotment. Because of the need for food, research is going on all the time to secure more disease-resistant strains to overcome inherent tendencies of plants to certain fungi, wilts and other maladies. Frequent replanting, particularly of those crops that become table-ready quickly, will lessen these destructive diseases.

December is the last page on the calendar, but there is no end to the garden year!

January

January is the beginning of a bright new year on the calendar, but it is the mid-month of winter. Perhaps nowhere is mythology more clearly demonstrated than in January, when we do indeed look backward to winter and forward to a promise of spring.

The new year steps forward

A whole bright year is before us! Let's make some New Year resolutions. Remember to enjoy the world about us while gardening by observing that the clods of newly turned earth are frosted white with ice each morning; that germinating seeds pushing up the crust of earth are mostly weeds; that pink-rimmed doughy white clouds come up above the mountains each afternoon and that the sound of children playing is a very happy thing.

New Year resolutions are often made in jest as the old year departs and the new one enters, but let there be no back-turning on the resolutions about your new garden this year. The calendar connotes more than a new year; it marks the beginning of a different garden season when winter turns its face toward spring. Consider the difference between the first two months (December and January) of the "dormant" season. In the beginning, days grow shorter, but by January's end they are showing signs of lengthening. We sense more warmth as the sun does a turnabout.

During the short days and long nights, when work may slack off, take time to become familiar with various groups of plants. Knowing many plants by name is comparable to having a wide knowledge of words.

Nature's crowning achievement

Consider the contribution to garden beauty flowering deciduous and evergreen trees make. If you choose carefully you may almost complete a year-long color calendar. It will be pleasant to sit in the cooling shade cast by the delicate fern-like foliage of either of these summer-flowering trees: the blue flowers of *Jacaranda acutifolia* echo the clear blue sky, and the pink tones of *Albizia julibrissin* chime in with the sunset's glow. This last is hardy almost anywhere, but if you plan to use crape myrtle with this pink-flowered acacia, choose white, palest pink or lavender for good color harmony—their bloom-time will overlap.

These medium-size trees will give high autumn color: sweet gum (liquidambar), Chinese pistache (*Pistacia chinensis*) or maidenhair fern tree (*Ginkgo biloba*). Choose sweet gum in autumn color if the diverse range of its autumn foliage is critical with other colors that may be in the garden at this time. These charming qualities make pistache my choice for a small tree: it gives harlequin effects for several late autumn weeks, is drought-enduring, disease and insect free, and with light shaping it may easily be fitted to even limited garden space and design. Rapid leaf-fall is another admirable trait of this nonfruiting tree.

Nature's etchings

Bare branches against a clear winter sky are as sharply drawn as a pen and ink sketch and reveal growth irregularities of V crotches, crossing branches, tying and staking defects and even dangerous injuries like the one shown on page 128, which is the result of using a nonrotting plastic-covered wire that was not loosened before the plant increased in girth and became "strangled" by the wire. Careful and expensive professional tree surgery may correct the condition, but attention to tying devices through the year and proper staking can prevent this injury.

Watch for next year's butterflies

Keep watch for various chrysalids—intricate incubators that contain next summer's enchanting butterflies—which may be found attached to small twigs by ever so delicate membranes of gossamer threads that support the dormant insect cradles through winter storms. With the first signs of returning spring warmth the shroud splits and an unbelievably large butterfly or moth emerges.

Summer-flowering trees need pruning now

Prune summer-flowering shrubs and trees. Cut out spent canes from climbing roses. Find time for small jobs, like pruning one tree, rose or vine, staking a few annuals, or looking over bulbs and roots that are stored to see how they are spending the winter.

Big jobs may be divided into units, such as digging one hole at a time for new roses, shrubs or trees. Until mild weather and pruning time return, fasten temporarily the wayward boughs of climbing vines and roses that may be damaged or broken by gusty winter winds.

Here is dramatic proof of what happens to trees that are left tied tightly to permanent stakes too long. During storms the tree often breaks off at one of the constrictions. Prevent this disaster by using a double-staking device, also shown in this chapter.

Look for your rainshadows

Rainshadows is the term geologists give land masses in the lee of mountain chains where rain falls in limited amounts. Man-made rainshadows may be found in many gardens and cause plant maladies that may not be obvious. They occur under permanent awnings, wide extended eaves, the lee side of buildings, dense evergreen shrubbery and leaf canopies that overhang the containers.

Other difficult locations are against south-facing walls with reflected heat that can raise the temperature considerably while other areas may be in complete shade. Modern architecture creates problem gardening regions.

To compensate for the conditions brought about by these rainshadows calls for extra care of soil, watering and feeding. During rains catch enough water to thoroughly leach salts from the soil that often accumulate with continued irrigation. Use organic soil-building plant foods and replenish humus as it loses bulk through decomposition.

Choose plants that have been proven hardy under these various and trying locations. Some attributes to look for are immunity to fungus diseases and not overly large leaves nor too rapid growth, all of which would make unsatisfactory plantings. Aspidistra in either the all-green or striped foliage and ferns with compact habit of growth come to mind for complete shade; *Euphorbia splendens* (crown-of-thorns) and complementary leaf forms of hardy succulents for sun are two plant groups that combine good looks with ease of culture. Hardiness takes on another meaning here—hardy to these trying physical conditions of location as well as extremes of temperature.

Study seasonal shadows

Then there are different kinds of shadows that vary from season to season. During these shortest days you may map the density and amount of shade in various beds and areas and make notes of plants to use next winter. Places that are all sun during summer's long days may be in complete shade now, and inversely, areas that are shaded in summer by deciduous trees may enjoy full winter sun. It all has to do with the sun's orbit through the seasons. A particularly trying area in winter is the north side of buildings, walls or large heavily foliaged plants. Some of those areas mentioned above may likewise have different exposures during winter's short days and low sun.

Keep the soil pH compatible

Group plants that need acid soil together. Convert an entire bed from neutral soil to a humusy root environment by removing a considerable amount of the soil and replacing it with a combination of peat moss and leaf mold or one of the composted forest waste products. Such a bed would be ideal for the ericas and azaleas. Hosta, the plantain lily, will add pleasant leaf contrast. Scottish heather does not take kindly to the arid atmosphere of warm latitudes but the ericas will give months of bloom. Try the four-foot-tall winter-blooming *Melanthera rosea*, and lower growing kinds to extend the flower calendar through several months. If it is not feasible to make a bed for acid-loving plants they will grow successfully in pots.

Feed all deciduous plants with manure, but wait until later when the roses have been pruned and sprayed to apply a manure dressing for pleasanter working conditions.

Even winter has its own work

Each garden season has its own peculiar work—planting, tending, harvest and enjoyment. Winter—the season with us now—is a most important one, when we lay down the foundation of the garden year. To see what is new and exciting visit nurseries and study new catalogs as they arrive. They are as truly harbingers of spring as bird migrations or the first crocus, and they may be studied at our leisure, but if that study doesn't result in an order for seeds, bulbs or plants they might as well never have come to the mail box.

January is often the wettest month, which means lower temperatures. Since days have been lengthening but a month, higher temperatures and renewed growth of plants are scarcely noticeable, and during this shortest-day period the lowest temperatures will be recorded. Don't just listen to nightly frost warnings, but take action. If you live in an area where the garden is not "bedded" for winter, either protect tender plants with coverings or bring those that are known to be exceptionally sensitive to low temperatures under shelter (see chapter 6).

Watch for tying damage

Check plant stakes and ties throughout the garden to make sure they are doing the job. Newly planted evergreen living Christmas trees will need to be firmly anchored to prevent blowing over in winter winds. By next year new roots will have grown to support the trees against storms.

Go over all plants that are kept staked, like tree roses, to be sure the supports are firm and that the ties have not cut into the bark or rotted away. Take advantage of a lull in winter storms to make holes for planting the alluring new roses, trees and shrubs that come bareroot. If old manure is available, blend some with the soil for gentle warmth to encourage new root growth, and to promote a healthy soil condition.

A vine for all reasons

Plants are the warp and woof of the garden's fabric and clothe it in a gracious many-hued tapestry that varies in texture and form. Vines are to the garden what grace notes are to music—delicate nuances that soften and provide a lilting quality. Vines may be grouped broadly as limber and structural (bold), with both deciduous and evergreen kinds included in each group. They bring seasonal color, screen storage areas and cover fences and arbors with graceful boughs and cooling shade.

The jasmines offer several with landscape values. *Jasmine grandiflorum* brings the first breath of springtime beauty with blooms shaded white to soft burgundy. Twining, evergreen *Trachelospermum jasminoides* continues the spring season with a canopy of star-like fragrant white flowers and shining foliage. Hardy *Chilean* or *Mandevilla jasmine* closes the autumn flower show before its abundant cool leaf curtains fall. Its intricate branches make spider-web shadow patterns on winter sunlit paving.

Large-flowered deciduous *Clematis* needs no champion, and will be remembered from a childhood spent in middle or eastern America, but *Clematis armandii* is not so well known, although it is hardy to 22° F. In spring its curtains of bloom are like a bride's train, and almost obscure the splendid evergreen foliage.

Limber vines are trailing, twining and draping. Honeysuckle, the jasmines, clematis and bignonias are excellent examples. The "creepers," both Boston ivy and Virginia creeper, combine both traits and are the gayest winter-leafed vines.

There is a vine for almost every effect, but choose wisely. Learn to prune for beauty and to train for screening, ground cover, drapery or whatever your landscape needs. Besides adding beauty, vines temper the atmosphere. In the shade of a plant-covered pergola, it may be 25° cooler than in unshaded areas. Plant foliage does more than cast shadows, it also reflects heat. Other plants with long vine-like boughs may be used to create charming cool garden retreats. Weeping mulberry almost heads the list, but bougainvillea, when grown over an umbrella-like structure, makes a charming colorful accent in the landscape. Wisteria will perform in like manner.

More shadow patterns

During this bareroot planting season consider the silhouettes various plants make. Shadows add a new dimension to garden design. Their reflections on lifeless paving add interest and subtlety with each changing season. Delicate lacy foliage casts light airy shadows, while trees with large luxuriant leaves give complete shade except at the branch tips, where the somber density may be relieved by some broken patterns.

A refresher on bareroot planting

It might be well to turn to chapter 6 and read the instructions about planting bareroot plants, but I will briefly go over the directions here. Make the holes wider than the outspread roots to provide freshly worked soil for new root growth. Keep the bud union of fruit trees and roses above the soil surface. Cut branches of roses down to six inches or so, and fruit trees back to eighteen to twenty-four inches, and snip any small side stems to one inch.

Choose one or two of the stronger new branches that may grow from the buds near the base of the shortened stems, and pinch off any others to grow a well-shaped tree. First aid for bareroot plants includes not letting roots become dry. Soaking overnight or for several hours in Vitamin B1 solution restores lost moisture to roots if they are not too dry to respond, but no amount of pampering can bring life to a dead plant. Learn to distinguish between a dormant plant whose cells are "asleep" and one that has suffered neglect to the point of decline.

Dry winters are often disastrous

Unseasonably high temperatures often occur in dry winters and may play havoc with newly set bareroot plants, particularly roses, unless some precaution is used to prevent early leafing before new roots have grown to supply the plant with moisture. A loose drape of porous cloth like burlap allows free air circulation, retards growth and prevents sunburn.

To prevent sunburn of newly set trees, paint the trunks with an *inside* water-base paint. This paint will cause less bark damage than outside water-base paint. Never use oil-base paint on living trees. Broken bark caused by sunburn may provide an easy entrance for borers. Because of the increase of a tree's girth, with consequent breaking of the protective paint, it is wise to renew the paint each year until the tree bark has grown tough enough to withstand the slanting rays of winter sun, usually about three seasons in the garden. Here an ounce of prevention is worth more than a pound of cure.

February

In this last month of winter look about for the noticeable signs of returning spring. Gain inspiration to tackle the prodigious weeding in your own garden by visiting a ravine or creek to enjoy the industry of bees filling their pollen baskets as they wallow among the emerging willow catkins.

Signs and sounds of spring

We know it is getting on toward spring when the cats, as if in mockery of the winter wind, howl around the house corners; only theirs are in rather shorter cadences. This month may see the end of heavy frost over much of our land. Do some planning for a colorful summer garden. Bring perfume to patio and outdoor living areas with potted and tubbed plants.

Although we may find visible signs of departing winter and returning spring, February is often a stormy month, as if Jupiter Pluvius was crowding the rest of winter together so spring can come through. With these storms in mind examine stakes and tying devices throughout the garden. Newly planted evergreens, not yet firmly rooted, may be blown over unless protected by firm stakes or windbreaks. Diligence will prevent plant injury or losses.

Even so, toward the end of the month many spring-like happenings will be recorded—flowers and vegetables planted last autumn will be ready to harvest, and add gaiety and eye appeal to house and table.

Advice for part-time gardeners

If you are a weekend/holiday gardener, try to make a quick tour of the garden each day, and on a stiff card jot down urgent jobs as they develop. This memorandum can be your Saturday schedule. Light chores may be done by the family gardener proficient with certain tasks, and arduous jobs shared by the family team. Tips to overcome fatigue are always welcome. Tools which are proper for the job and the right size for you contribute to tireless gardening.

Use the right tool for the right job

Sprained backs, lame shoulders and arm muscles that require doctors' adjustment on Mondays are reputed to be 50 percent of the time the result of using tools incorrectly or the wrong tools just because they were handy.

Are you a pushover for garden gadgets? Convenience tools are as necessary to carefree gardening as they are in the kitchen, but often I find the gadgeteer with a box or basket piled so full of these one-job things it's discouraging to look for the right one. So, the gardener goes about his piled so full of these one-job things it's discouraging to look for the right one. So, the gardener goes about his weekend chores with round-pointed shovel, sturdy spading fork, perhaps a hoe and I hope a steel rake, and, protruding from his hip pocket, the most-used and easily his favorite tool, an asparagus cutter.

Being a lifelong gardener, I'd be the last to affirm that the right tool will take the labor out of gardening, only that it makes it less laborious. Basic tools have evolved through trial and error, but they are as functional as hands; if used wisely they can avert injury to both man and plant, make gardening less strenuous and more enjoyable and save money in the doing.

Shovels and spading forks are for making planting holes and loosening soil in preparation for planting. Hoes are for weeding and making furrows in previously prepared soil. Bamboo rakes are excellent to gather light litter into piles but useless to rake lumpy soil smooth. Small hand tools, trowels, etc., should be used only for their size job—like setting young plants.

There are many uses for hedge shears other than pruning hedges. They are excellent for lopping off old blooms on small bedding plants, snipping weeds that occur among plants that may not be hoed safely, or renovating the strawberry ground cover if it is not too extensive (in which case use the lawnmower set as high as it will go to avoid injury to plant crowns).

For the light task of thinning young seedlings my favorite tool is a pair of kitchen utility scissors. Snip the plants near the ground, and they will not grow again, and, best of all, you avoid having to firm soil around plants that are to remain when plants are pulled.

Rodents are active

It is about time for the gopher population explosion. One female caught now means at least a half-dozen less to cope with this spring and a prodigious number less by summer's end. One way to outsmart these nocturnal varmints is to line planting holes with inch mesh chicken netting. But to get rid of them keep traps working. They are not storing food now so poison grain is wasted, but poison carrots may prove enticing. Place these well within the burrow.

Yet another nocturnal garden inhabitant is the common mole. The different earth work of moles and gophers is easy to detect. Mole runs are barely subsurface and may be tramped shut or beaten down with a shovel to prevent roots drying out. Gopher workings are finely pulverized mounds of soil thrown up on tunneling from one choice plant to another. Vegetarian field mice find good pickings in choice bulbs and roots in open tunnels the carnivorous mole makes in skirting around, under or otherwise exposing plant roots in their search for grubs and insects. Moles are therefore beneficial, while gophers serve no worthwhile purpose. In either case, act promptly to save plants. Vigilance is the trump card that saves plants and water, which is often wasted down the network of gopher runways, instead of being used by plants.

Gardeners in temperate zones need to be diligent to prevent rodent damage to plants protected by winter overcoats. One safeguard is to place rodent control beneath the winter covering before installing it (see chapter 6).

Catch up on work for spring

Lift waterlily tubs if this was not done in autumn. Work over the roots as you do iris, and replant in new soil. Containers for waterlily roots should be a minimum of two feet square and a foot deep. Fill two-thirds with manure, and plant the roots in sod-soil to prevent muddying the pool. To ensure longer life of wooden containers for these aquatic beauties paint inside and outside to retard decay. Use an asphalt-base wood preservative, not coal tar, which may burn plant roots. Give other wood tubs the same inside treatment, and paint the bottom outside.

Bareroot plants are plentiful now, and less expensive than they will be later; also, a better selection of kinds and quality is offered. If you are looking for a fast-growing deciduous tree to sit under this summer, consider two that come bareroot. Fruitless mulberry carries a canopy of large, dark green leaves while *Albizia julibrissin* has cool fern-like foliage and is topped all summer with a pink haze of acacia-like bloom. Both are wide-branched to form a sylvan retreat, and drought-resistant as well as hardy.

Complete planting of all bareroot trees, shrubs, roses, vines and perennial vegetables by the end of this month. If the winter is dry, water frequently enough to maintain good health. While the plants are apparently dormant, life processes such as new root growth begin soon after planting.

Prune roses now

Pruning follows upon the heels of dormant planting or may even precede it, as weather, time and individual preferences permit.

Buds on rose bushes and canes of climbers should be plump enough to make pruning visually easy. Study the plant, decide upon the best wood to keep and plan for new spring growth. It is important to remember that bush roses bloom on new wood, while climbers bloom out of year-old canes. When most of the buds along the canes have produced flower stems, remove the cane entirely to the crown; or if more canes are needed, cut those old spent canes down to a strong dormant bud—about two feet from the ground. This should force out those dormant buds into vigorous new canes that will be flowering wood for next season's display. If we learn to manage climbing roses they can be a charming landscape feature, but let nature dominate and you will have a tangled, unproductive canebreak.

Late winter is traditionally rose-pruning time, but if it is practiced throughout the year until late autumn, flowers should be available except in the three winter months, and even in open winters Christmas roses are not unusual. If we use wise judgment in cutting flowers, give frequent feeding, and allow time in late autumn for wood maturity, there won't be that "slaughter" so abhorred by many rose growers, and you will not come to the stalemate of unproductiveness seen in so many rose gardens.

To learn more about pruning roses attend rose-pruning demonstrations by garden clubs or other groups to learn new

Right and wrong ways to prune branches

1. Cut too slanting; bud will not receive enough moisture from the sap flow to continue to grow.

2. Cut too far above the bud; branch will probably die, not only back to the bud but will continue down the branch through the cambium layer of cells. Quite prevalent in rose pruning.

3. Cut is made too close to the bud, not allowing enough wood to support the new growth.

4. A correct cut, which will heal readily, or produce a strong branch for a rose or new growth to continue the tree.

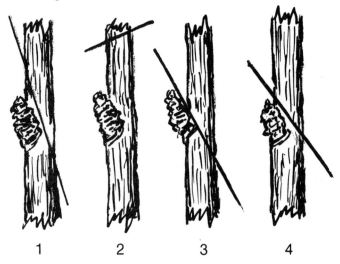

1   2   3   4

techniques and old proven theories. But here are a few suggestions to ponder: remove interfering branches, or if one is needed, separate them with twisted withes (see chapter 1), and cut out all weak growth. Retain no more than five to seven strong canes even in older established plants to allow for air circulation. The results of leaving too many robust canes will be either a proliferation of weak growth inside the plant or fewer new canes developing from dormant buds along the canes; both result in inferior blooms, mildew and rust.

General pruning tips

Learn to prune with and for a purpose. Study each plant's individual growth habit, producing time and the way flowers and/or fruit are borne and at what season. Some plants flower on new wood, some on mature (last season) wood and others on short thorny projections called fruit spurs that continue to bear fruit or flowers for several years.

Here is help for tree pruning: study the tree and mark branches you think should be removed with conspicuous cloth strips before beginning work. Then work slowly and observe the effect each cut makes on the shape and strength of the future tree. Remember, if you cut to a bud branches will sprout along the stem, but prune to a branch for control of size (see chapter 6).

Lifetime school for gardeners

Lifetime learning is more than a catch phrase. I like to ponder its many facets from time to time as it applies to gardening. In a summer-dry climate a sixth sense will be a guide in wise water use. Choose plants suited to the region and use mulches along with ground covers to conserve moisture and to enhance the beauty of the garden. Don't mix plants with different water needs. Ornamental strawberry makes a luxuriant informal ground cover, and *Arctostaphylos uva-ursi* (bearberry) is native to wide climate regions. Other indigenous plants will suggest themselves once the idea of easier garden maintenance takes hold.

As summer approaches with its long water routine, consider replacing high-moisture-need plants with those that can withstand drought. Drought-enduring plants are not a sad compromise for more conventional kinds. They are the answer to a long-sought way to landscape gardens with material that requires the least amount of supplemental moisture and effort to grow.

A farewell to winter is premature

A burst of warm weather this month may seem like spring is near, but we must cater to winter at least until mid-March when lengthening days will bring stronger sun warmth. Before you turn loose of winter complete these chores: bareroot planting, pruning before buds begin to break ("dormant" pruning, not evergreen plants); and spraying of all deciduous fruits and roses. Bordeaux compound (dormant strength), a copper formula, is safe for all deciduous fruits and roses, does not stain redwood walls or fences as lime-sulfur may, and is just as effective (see chapter 6).

As outside work begins in earnest, work to lessen fatigue. If you tire in one part of your body beyond normal fatigue, watch your work habits. See that you have correct posture, rhythm, and proper tools for the job. Experiment humming tunes with various meters to set the pace for different jobs, as the sailors of old worked the great sailing ships.

Population explosion occurs in gardens too

Where a plant has gone to seed, young plants spring up thick if there is space for them. Prick off those you wish to keep and to share with friends and weed out the rest, then replant where you intend for them to flower. Overcrowding means undernourishment and promotes disease. Slugs and snails, sow and pillbugs also find the dark moist shade of plants a perfect retreat. Use specific bait for control.

Even with the help of small bird seed-harvesters, larkspur and other easily grown annuals produce thick stands of volunteer plants from self-sown seed; only by ruthless thinning can young plants achieve worthwhile flowering. The fleeting quality of annuals makes them unsuited to the main display areas of the garden, but in limited space there often isn't any other place, so we make the best of what we have

and enjoy their exuberant color. The old custom of growing
annuals for bouquet flowers in the vegetable garden was not
only practical, but made the mundane vegetable garden a plot
of perfumed beauty and color.

For continuous color grow perennial Isaac House *scabiosa*,
a delightful flower for cutting. Lobelia is a gay border edging
and a welcome change from annual alyssum; it will last longer
and comes in white, red, and light and dark blue.

Spring is on its way

This month will be the first showing in markets of easy-
to-grow spring bulbs. Choose *Babiana* for a bluest blue, *ixia*,
Leucojum vernum, sparaxis, Tigridia (often called Mexican
daylily), and pink calla lily roots. These last two will make
colorful movable pot plants.

Plants to provide color and food in the spring garden
should be kept well nourished. The advantage of concentrated
plant food with a known analysis—either chemical or
organic—is that you may almost predict the results each time
it is used.

Unless we are diligent, even established plants may suffer
for water when the winter is dry, because the earth absorbs
the moisture from their roots. Evergreens announce their
water need with drooping leaves, while the bare branches of
deciduous plants are mute; nonetheless, their moisture need is
equally urgent. To determine soil moisture, check various
areas of the garden with shovel or spading fork. Watering the
garden in winter calls for extra care. If temperatures in your
area fall below freezing, hoses will need to be unscrewed and
drained after each use to be free of ice next morning.

As in house cleaning, there are two schools of thought in
fighting garden insects. Do a little each day, don't let it get
ahead of you; or go nonchalantly through summer, autumn,
winter and have one *big* spring clean-up; leave no stone or
other hiding place unturned, unsprayed, unbaited. I am of the
"little at a time" school, feeling that in this way I can keep
chewers like slugs, snails, sowbugs and earwigs under control.

Keep close watch for first signs of mildew on garden and
sweet pea foliage and stock, and rust on snapdragon plants.

Prevention is the key word here, rather than control (see chapter 6).

Grow gourmet vegetables

An advantage of a home garden is that expensive foods cost no more to grow. Perennial vegetables that come back each year are profitable. Asparagus goes dormant, but green globe artichokes' bold sculptured foliage is at its best during winter, and gets shaggy as it takes a rest after the energetic production of the delicious "chokes." Cut the old leaves back to the ground, and new luxuriant foliage will come out soon. The bright red stems of rhubarb (pie plant) are a striking feature of the spring garden. Rhubarb chard is a welcome change from the green kind—more healthful and delicious either cooked or in salads.

Where weather is favorable this may be the best month to begin an early spring vegetable garden. Bush peas sown now should reach perfection before mildew weather comes. Root vegetables planted last fall will be ready for use now, and be in prime quality for the freezer. This adjunct to our food preservation program is a great boon to vegetable and fruit growers. By freezing we not only enjoy out-of-season vegetables, but actually save time and precious space by growing surpluses during the best season for them and freezing them for later use. This saves growing a complete garden at one time, and makes crop rotation more possible (see table in chapter 2).

In all but colder regions, each day sees some exciting bursting forth, which may portend either good or evil, depending upon our role as nature's assistants, and whether we are studying insect life in the garden or aiming for a bumper harvest of flowers and vegetables. To be a successful gardener calls for a certain interest in and knowledge of insect ways. Working to keep control is a happier attitude than fretting about extermination, which is almost impossible and perhaps not even desirable. For instance, a sterile garden would not provide insect food for birds, certainly one of the enjoyable side benefits of tending a garden.

Winter, for all its somber look, is the prelude to awakening nature. Whether it's a long deep sleep, as in the far

North, or a catnap, as in the warm latitudes, it is a season to be anticipated, reveled in and loved for what it brings. Each temperature zone will of course have a different day for spring's arrival and the beginning of the garden year.

This verse expresses perfectly the seasons as gardeners experience them:

> *"Autumn to winter, winter into spring,*
> *spring into summer, summer into fall,*
> *so rolls the changing year, and so we*
> *change—motion so swift, we know not*
> *that we move . . ."*
>
> D. M. Mulock

Part II

A Clear
and Simplified Method
of Gardening

Work centers are essential to the business of gardening. The pot rack above, and cupboards below a work table hold extra flats, soil screens, etc.

An elegant work center where one may carry on several activities. Potting materials are kept under the work bench in closed cupboards. Flower-arranging vases and tools of the trade are within arm's reach. The bold shadow pattern on the paving is cast by the conical roof made of split wood, the same as the walls of the structure.

Chapter 5
Organization

Getting started

When is a good time to begin a garden? Anytime. The main thing is to begin. If your home is acquired during the dormant time of year, you could begin with armchair gardening, but not the kind that is synonymous with drooling over pictures of incredibly perfect flowers, fruits and vegetables growing in impeccable gardens. The kind of armchair gardening that is needed includes planning with paper, pencil, T square, plant dictionaries, and seed catalogs. Actually, if more of that kind of armchair gardening were done before beginning the dirt gardening, the what, where and when of the garden you visualize would become a reality much sooner.

Frustration with gardening comes largely from lack of forethought and planning. There is no royal road to creating a garden. Backaches, heartaches and moneyaches are all a part of getting started. We hear "experience is the best teacher," but kindly guidance can help avoid much of the doing-over waste of beginning gardeners.

A budget can eliminate some wild extravagances often indulged in by both members of the team. He is generally a pushover for new tools, when what the garden may need most is food. She is just as foolish about plants currently in bloom. How few jobs some clever gadget may be used for may not occur to him, or where she will plant the charming thing with the exotic flowers may not occur to her. Don't go off on any wild buying sprees until the garden is well established.

Look behind the scenes to learn what will be needed to make the inviting garden you've been planning. First may be good soil (you may need to buy yards of it), humus to conserve moisture and to create a good growing medium, and well-started healthy permanent landscape plants. You'll also need insecticides and applicators for their effective use.

The business of gardening can be made easier if adequate tools and equipment to work with are at hand. Convenient work areas in which to do the many little projects that come up in an average day or weekend of the busy gardener, such as potting or seed sowing, can be a genuine joy.

Does your garden say "enjoy" or "get busy"? Working in the garden is enjoyable, but rest and contemplation are also worthy of consideration. Learn to organize the garden work to allow time for relaxation.

Take a brief turn around the garden before beginning work to discover what is happening and what needs most to be done. Those few moments in the garden before beginning work will be time well spent, if you take along a stiff card and soft pencil to jot down the things that are to be done. Each task will require special planning and tools. Don't, however, lay out more than you can do easily, for in that way lies discouragement, frustration and overtiredness. This tour of inspection will give a plan of action. You will know just what to do, so get busy!

First, collect the tools necessary to the work, not forgetting the right kind of gloves. It will speed the work considerably to have a garden basket which should contain the necessary small tools: trowels, scratchers, shears, saw and several kinds of tying material—raffia, string, twists, labels

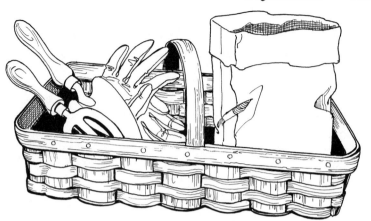

Don't go into the garden empty-handed, but putter with a purpose. A commodious split-wood basket goes with me on my early morning rounds; saves many steps, finger nails and temper. Best of all, it gets small jobs done. Include a stiff card and pencil for memos or thoughts as well as work to be done. A large litter bag is added convenience.

and pencil. Having these small tools handy will save many steps and assure a more systematic method of work.

The sequence of work is important. Prune (or clip), harvest, feed, then water is a logical routine. Afterwards, put out bait for whatever seems most prevalent—slugs, snails, sowbugs—and also spray or dust when foliage is dry enough not to dilute the insecticide unduly.

Tools and equipment

Tools are a long-lasting investment. Do not confuse the things you work with with those you use up, which are supplies. Some of the tools and equipment listed here you may not need at once if you are beginning a new project. Get the basic tools first, and add other equipment as the need for them becomes apparent.

Work tools

Clippers (various sizes), loppers and pruning saw, cart or wheelbarrow, hoe, rake, spade, spading fork, hay fork for weeds and grasses, shovel.

Weeding devices

Mowers, cutters, sickle, asparagus cutter, light mattock, short-handled hoe, scuffle hoe, spading fork, kneeling pad, strong knife, scissors.

Maintenance tools

Lawn and/or weed mowers, sprayers and dusters to apply insecticides; files, carborundum stone, oil can, wire brush. Two rags in cans —one impregnated with oil, the other with furniture polish for tools and tool handles.

Equipment

Sun and wind sheltering devices for protection. Glass and burlap to cover seed boxes, flats, pots; watering can (place the sprinkling head in the can when using as a filling device, so you will always know where it is). Labels, pencil, garden record book, hammer, hatchet, stakes, string for marking rows. A six-by-six-foot square of canvas and a bushel basket or box for weeds. A broom and various tying materials— raffia, (cut into usable lengths), horticultural twine, gloves, twist-ems. Learn to work in gloves. Cloth-lined plastic gloves are excellent for most chores, and a boon for busy gardeners, but for laying brick paving or stone walls and rose pruning, heavier leather ones afford more protection.

Gardening in safety is more than a slogan. Rakes and hoes left with their teeth or blades up may be stepped on and are as dangerous as a serpent. Handles may be broken, and may cause injury to yourself or to your helper. Tools lying down are difficult to see, and may be missed when putting things away at the close of a busy work session.

Tools will last for years if given ordinary care; they should be kept under cover when not in use. When storing them for the winter, or when the need arises, renovate handles and metal parts with oil and polish. Sand handles lightly whenever splinters appear.

Using tools only for the work they are designed to do will not only make the work easier, but tools last longer. The rhythm of work and swing of the whole body can be

Nail keg work-tool keeper, may be fashioned from any other wood container.

wonderful exercise. Using the wrong tool can be quite a muscle binder-upper and can ruin the tool. Some common errors: digging holes in hard ground with a trowel when a shovel or pick would be better, cutting too large branches with hand shears or even loppers when a saw is needed for the job, or using shears as a trowel.

One way to avoid much of this kind of work is to keep the seasonal small tools in a garden basket, and take it along with you, wherever you are working. Select those things that are pertinent to the day's work to lighten the weight. In this way, shears, gloves, kneeling pad and other items are always at hand, and handy. If they are returned to the basket when a task is done, they are not so likely to be lost, or left behind. One idea is illustrated above.

151

Chapter 6
Planting and Maintenance

Dirt + organic matter = soil

Soil is the most important element in the world. Civilization and life itself depend upon it. Yet how gardeners abuse it. They flood it, leaching valuable food elements below the feeder roots, work it when too wet or allow it to cake hard before attempting to cultivate.

Gardeners work from the ground up. If plants are to thrive the soil must be right. We must learn to manage the soil, and how to change it to meet different plants' needs. The physical and chemical aspects of the soil are equally important. Most soils need humus to improve the physical character. Both conditions can be modified by the kind of humus used.

Very tight soils (clay and adobe) need to be loosened to create air spaces. Light (porous, sandy) soils can be made loamy by the addition of organic substances—barnyard manure, hay, straw or other inexpensive additives—to create a favorable root habitat.

The pH requirements vary for deciduous and evergreen plants. It is the symbol used to measure the rudiments of soil chemistry. A soil's pH depends upon the degree to which it is acid, neutral or alkaline. Cranberry, peat and sphagnum bogs represent the lowest acid soil condition—pH 4. A pH of 6 is the soil needed by most splendid broad-leafed evergreen plants. A pH of 7—normal soil—neither acid nor alkaline, is suited to average field and garden plants, deciduous fruits and shrubs. At the alkaline limits of plant tolerance—pH 9, only desert plant life survives.

There are two fundamental plant groups. They are either evergreen and retain their leaves year-round, or they drop their leaves seasonally and are called deciduous. The evergreens have either broad leaves or needle-like foliage. Because broad leaves have a luxuriant subtropical aspect they are associated with warm latitudes. While this is not always so, it is true in great measure, since they do not shed ice and snow as readily as deciduous plants, those with reduced foliage, or conifers—the cone bearers.

The pH scale is used here to show the acid-alkaline needs of a few plant groups and how they can be fitted into our gardens by correcting, where needed, the soil chemistry. When related to the text it should be relatively easy to succeed with different kinds of plants. Further information on plant feeding and how to achieve proper soil chemistry will be found in Chapter 6.

pH scale for measuring soil chemistry

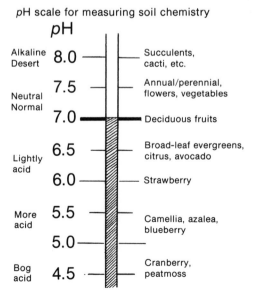

pH		
Alkaline Desert	8.0	Succulents, cacti, etc.
Neutral Normal	7.5	Annual/perennial, flowers, vegetables
	7.0	Deciduous fruits
Lightly acid	6.5	Broad-leaf evergreens, citrus, avocado
	6.0	Strawberry
More acid	5.5	Camellia, azalea, blueberry
	5.0	
Bog acid	4.5	Cranberry, peatmoss

Evergreen plants require an acid soil, which in their native habitat is created from their own fallen leaves. The soft, deep-pile carpet we tread upon in a forest is a combination of animal life and decaying vegetable mold.

Plants native to woodlands where the soil is high in humus have fibrous, even hair-like roots that are adequate to supply them with food that is in solution in the free soil moisture. Azalea and fern roots are good examples of this type.

If the basic soil of an area is alkaline, or even neutral, a bed can be fixed to meet the acid needs of plants by adding about 50 percent by bulk of peat moss and leaf mold. Peat moss acidity is of utmost importance when preparing beds for acid-loving plants. The combination is better than either element alone. The finer peat moss will fill the gaps between the coarser leaf mold particles, and since it is practically immune to decay will remain an important component longer than leaf mold, which in a few years will decompose into rich, loamy soil. As this occurs fresh peat moss and leaf mold should be added to keep the original soil level in the beds.

Then, if acid-reacting plant foods are used the acid requirements of plants are usually maintained, but under extreme alkaline conditions it may be necessary to use a soil acidifier in addition to acid-reacting foods; either soil sulfur or agricultural gypsum will be satisfactory. Cottonseed meal is a complete organic acid-reacting plant food with satisfactory analysis for plant growth. In some western states the parent soil is often alkaline, and irrigation water may be also. Under these conditions acid plant foods are important even for average garden plants.

Some areas have a climate favorable to broad-leafed evergreens, but often not the soil. It is easier to change the soil both physically and chemically than to modify the weather. By correct soil preparation and feeding programs, luxuriant subtropical effects can be achieved in a country that has desert tendencies, to say the least.

Plants of the open plains and mesas will thrive with less organic matter in the soil than those native to wooded areas. Large deciduous trees require less humus, but remember, nature provides a decaying mat of leaves for the plants' well-being. It is insulation against summer drought and winter cold. It holds the rainfall and melting snow that ensures deep watering.

Soil of an evergreen orchard or grove or even under a single large tree is almost always shaded, and therefore cooler and a better habitat for soil organisms than a deciduous plant where the sun dries out the soil, at least for a portion of the year.

We seldom find the same permanent, thick mat of leaf mold in a deciduous forest that we associate with an evergreen one, partly because deciduous leaves are generally lighter in texture. Thus the drying action of sun and wind tends to dehydrate deciduous leaves so completely that there is little fiber left to decay and mold.

This is the difference we face between the two groups of plants. The more we apply this knowledge of plants' requirements to our own small home garden, the more successful we will be. By planting evergreens where they can enjoy a cool root run, we can by using acid-reacting mulches soon give their roots a bacterial condition similar to that of their native habitat.

The one soil condition to avoid, if at all possible, is that of poor drainage, often encountered in low-lying land. Sometimes drain tile may be laid to carry excess water to a lower level, or toward a storm drain. Factors that contribute to a too-wet soil condition are: underlying hardpan or an impervious substratum, excess drainage into the plot from some other area, and just plain carelessness in water management during irrigation. This last condition is of course much easier to control.

Other points to observe in the selection of a site for a garden include the former use of the land. Old vegetable fields may have a high nematode population, so that soil fumigation may be not only helpful but necessary. This combined with care in choosing nematode-resistant plants or varieties may assure a modicum of success. Deciduous fruit trees are grown on nematode-resistant root stock.

Subsoiling may be important where an area is heavily infested with rodent burrows, or where there may be a plow sole as a result of many years of cultivation. Diligent control measures carried on throughout the year will certainly show results in reducing the number of plants eaten off by underground enemies. See the section on rodents in this chapter.

Choosing and planting dormant (bareroot) plants
and those from containers and balled-in-burlap (BB)

During winter and early spring many kinds of deciduous plants may be purchased without soil on their roots, or packed in moss, at considerable saving. It is of utmost importance that the stock be No. 1 grade. The buds of trees and shrubs should be plump and the bark smooth when lightly rubbed with the thumb. The short stems of berry plants should be alive and pliable, with new branch buds showing at the root crown. Perennial plants should have healthy crown leaves and their roots should not be dry. In fact, moist roots are perhaps the high point to look for. *Protect from drying out* should be the watchword until bareroot nursery stock is planted.

If ornamental trees have short branches, cut those back to within two or three inches of the stem or trunk, but not off completely. Dormant buds at the base of the branches will in all probability break into strong branches. After this growth comes out, retain the stronger and pinch off the weak ones. Space the branches around the stem of the tree by cutting off those that might make V crotches later on. These opposite branches are not only weak structurally, but form a pocket where debris may lodge and create a wet condition. Rotting sometimes begins there early in the life of the tree and causes splitting in later years.

The following suggestions for the treatment of bareroot plants after they are in your garden may get you off to a good start. If I didn't know gardeners so well, I might hope that you would have the holes dug, and the stakes for the new plants lying by them complete with tying materials and labels, but since this isn't likely, here is something important to do while making the holes. Don't be in a big rush to plant, because "haste surely makes for waste" in planting.

Prepare a quantity of water for soaking. I find an old wash tub almost indispensable in gardening, but few persons have them nowadays. However, most do own a wheelbarrow or metal garden cart to make a solution; soak the plant's roots for several hours before setting out. Regardless of what some people say I know I have better results if I soak bareroot plants in vitamin B1 or some other shock-reducing preparation before planting. This does more than reduce shock, it encourages root growth, and goes a long way toward protecting roots against immediate infection by soil-borne organisms, and replaces moisture that might have been lost by the plant in transportation from the growing fields to you.

Prune off any broken and excessively long roots and branches at this time. Holes for planting are of primary importance. They should be of adequate size for roots. A hole for a tree in fair soil should be at least six inches wider all around than the outspread roots. Poor rocky soil presents a different problem and poorly drained soil still another.

Consider these soils one at a time. Poor rocky soil should be removed from a considerable excavation—about three feet across and as deep. Test for drainage. If water stands for more than a day, place at least six inches of coarse gravel in the bottom for drainage. Then use good soil for planting. Often poor drainage is found even in rocky soil; the texture will determine this. If the soil between the rocks is sandy or porous you will have good drainage, but if it is heavy and sticky when wet poor drainage may result. It has been found better to condition the heavy soil that is taken from the hole rather than refill with lighter soil which may absorb water more freely than the surrounding earth and create a condition similar to planting in a container without holes for seepage. Heavy soil may be lightened by using agricultural gypsum (in the West) at about three pounds per cubic foot of soil, and lime in the acid soil belt of the East. Soil for filling and planting should approximate that of the field or garden in texture.

Diverting excessive runoff of water from the root areas of trees will often compensate for lack of drainage. To facilitate watering, the soil about individual trees is frequently a little lower than the surrounding ground. During excessive rainfall water may collect in the basins and drown a plant almost before we realize it.

In regions where the principal rainfall comes in winter while plants are dormant, filling the slight depressions with earth and breaking the berm or ridge of soil placed around the tree to hold summer irrigation water will help in preventing a surplus water supply while the plant is resting.

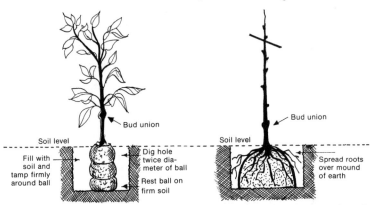

A typical bareroot tree shown in simulated planting situation. After the hole is made, shovel in enough soil to form a mound. Firm well to prevent settling, which would pull the new plant too low into the soil. Carefully measure the height from the root crown to the bud union or graft; keep it 3 inches above normal ground line. Use these precautions when planting roses and all other budded and/or grafted plants. Those balled in burlap or container-grown are of course not set upon a mound, because the soil is not removed from their roots.

Consider the actual planting process. The cutaway sketches here show how both bareroot plants and those from containers or balled in burlap should be set in the holes. The usual admonition to spread out the plant's roots over a mound of soil does not take into account different root types. We are obliged to plant a shrub or tree to conform to the root pattern or design. Some plants have a fine network of roots that may be spread out while others have merely a long taproot. But even with this latter root structure, a wide hole should be made for new feeder roots to grow into as they develop. Of course, plants that come from containers are planted at the prescribed depth, as are trees or shrubs that come balled in either burlap or moss.

All budded (grafted) plants—fruit trees and roses—should be set so the bud is always well above the soil to prevent sucker growth which might kill the fruiting or flowering portion of the plant.

I belong to the *no tromp* school of tree planters, preferring to settle the soil over the roots with water. After it has seeped away, divide the solution in which the plants were soaked among the plants. Follow this with a mulch of finely pulverized soil to completely fill the hole. Top off with a blanket of old manure or hay to maintain an even temperature and to prevent the soil drying out and baking, and the plant is off to a good start. It may be advisable to mound earth around the crown or bud union six to eight inches high when planting to prevent damage from extremes of temperature. Be sure to remove the mound to the ground level, however, as the buds begin to break in spring to avoid suckering.

Planting in containers—in the out-of-doors

You don't need to be a scientific climatologist or wizard to grow thrifty plants; however, a feel for and rapport with their growth needs is essential. This in substance is what is known as a *green thumb*. Growing skill comes through experience, learning through trying, joy through accomplishment. Think small like your garden, but high like your hopes!

Potting techniques are much like open ground planting, except that here you are dealing with contained soil, and the relation of root to pot size is a factor in growing thrifty plants. Don't overpot! The new pot should be no more than twice the size of the one the plant is growing in, or a three-inch size for transplanted seedlings.

Observe the same precautions with budded plants (roses and fruits) as in open ground planting. Keep the graft or bud above the permanent soil line. Nonbudded plants, cuttings or seedlings may be set deeper, tipped to one side, and more than one planted in a container or other variations to create a desired effect. When potting cover the holes with a bit of broken pot, screen wire or small flat stone for drainage and to prevent soil sifting out. An excess of gravel in the pot may give too much drainage. After all, water should be contained in the pot, not run out the bottom. The cutaway sketch and captions here will explain the process.

Soil is important and can mean the difference between success and failure. Prepared potting soil that is readily available is a good buy and saves time and labor; also for small operations one does not need to get quantities of different elements in order to get started with gardening. Potting soil, whether for individual containers or planters, may contain 50 percent humus. Soil loses considerable bulk through decomposition of the humus and will need to be replenished with fresh soil mix to maintain the soil level. Next to using correct soil comes water, which is discussed thoroughly in the section on Watering Methods in chapter 7.

Repotting diagram

Observe the technique used here to repot a good-sized fern. The old soil ball is set deep enough to cover the top of the old soil. A potting stick is used to firm the new soil-mix against the old pot side to encourage new root growth.

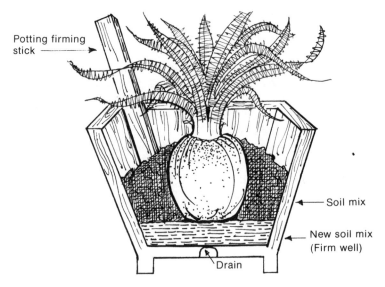

Potting firming stick

Soil mix

New soil mix (Firm well)

Drain

Creating a strawberry barrel

It is just as practical to grow fruits and vegetables in containers as ornamentals. Strawberries grown in jars and barrels add a different dimension to garden landscapes. The design shown here has been well tested and will ensure high production. Follow these steps to a successful venture.

Because barrels come in about as many sizes as people, it is a good idea to get the container first and fit the plant to it. These popular planters vary from the decorative ceramic strawberry jars through nail kegs to 50-gallon wooden barrels. The design shown and described here is made with a 35-gallon size barrel.

Hardwood barrels are best because they resist decay, and if they have been charred inside it is not necessary to treat them, except the outside of the bottom. Softwood barrels that were used for liquids other than oils, tar or other corrosives are satisfactory provided they are given a coat of asphalt emulsion on inside and outside of the bottom to retard decay.

Mechanical contrivances to rotate the barrel are not necessary. It can be turned easily with aid of a dolly. Although strawberry plants are hardy to several degrees below freezing, during an extremely cold spell it may be advisable to protect the planter. One easy way is to cover it with canvas held a foot or so above the barrel by sticks stuck into the soil of the barrel. Since these planters are portable to a degree, in extremely severe climates they may be moved under shelter for the winter.

The author shows essential steps to follow in making a successful strawberry barrel. The planting areas are marked, some already out, the three-
quarter-inch holes are drilled for coping saw to enter. Work is in progress.

How to begin—designing the barrel

With a tape measure, find out how large the barrel is at the middle. Space the holes eight inches apart on centers, give or add an inch. Since barrels are slightly smaller at the ends, those holes will be a bit nearer together. Offset the holes for harmony of design and to give maximum root space and full light to the plants. Make holes for drainage below the last course of planting spaces near the bottom, or in the bottom.

Make a three-inch triangular pattern and outline the cutouts with chalk. Bore three-quarter inch holes at the corners for the coping saw to enter. Triangular holes are easier to saw by hand than round ones, but if a power tool is available round ones do not present a problem. However, holes smaller than three inches do not allow for aeration of the soil and for the growth of plants. Holes that are too small are a common cause of failure.

A watering column (see picture) is necessary to evenly moisten the soil during the life of the plants. From a piece of metal screen wire form a four-inch column as long as the barrel is deep. Fill with sand at the same time the barrel is filled with soil to keep the pressure equal. Liquid plant food may be added through the sand when the plants show the need of nourishment, or in early spring and again toward summer's end in anticipation of late berries.

Place the wire column in the center of the barrel and hold it upright with strings. You are now ready to proceed with the excitement of planting.

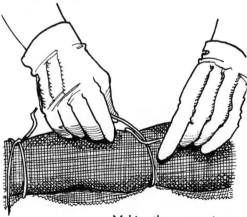

Making the screen wire watering column.

Getting ready to plant

Because strawberry plants are quite perishable, if you are using bareroot plants it is good growth insurance to set them out in a box of soil for new roots to form. Set the box in half shade and keep the soil moist. When young leaves begin to show in the crown it is a sign your plants are alive and well, and it is all right to begin planting. It is important to get a variety that is hardy and tested for your area. Everbearing kinds are usually preferred because they yield again through late summer and fall following the heavy spring crop. It's a good plan to buy a few extra plants to allow for possible losses.

Work on the barrel is complete; watering column in place, ready to begin planting. A two-year-old barrel in flourishing production may be seen in the *Spring* section at the beginning of this book. This production provides the author with an abundant harvest for several weeks in spring and with an everbearing variety a repeat performance may be enjoyed in late summer.

Soil for planting

Get enough soil to fill the planter plus some extra for firming and settling. You may use either prepared mix or blend your own, but in either case add one quart super-phosphate to each bushel of soil, and add one part sharp sand to the ready mix. If you choose to blend your own soil this is a good formula: equal parts sharp sand (not ocean beach), loam and composted humus, one-fourth part old manure. Get enough extra sand to fill the watering column. Blend the soil elements thoroughly. If the mix seems dry it may be moistened by a few quick swishes of a sprinkler while blending. It is a good idea to get the soil ready before beginning the project to allow it to mellow while you are building the barrel.

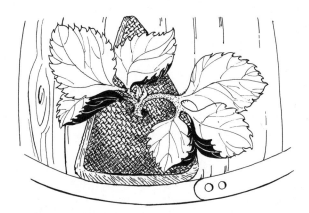

A simulated planting diagram of a strawberry plant in a burlap planting square, held in one of the barrel openings. In addition to feeding with liquid plant food through the watering column, concentrated plant food tablets may be pushed into the soil alongside of each plant.

Planting

Cut from burlap or other coarse cloth one eight-inch square for each plant. Make a small slit near the center of each square just large enough to bring the plant leaves through. These pieces of cloth are used to prevent soil sifting out while the plants are growing to fill the soil.

Fill the container to the first row of holes, and firm gently. Add a shovelful of soil near each hole to use in setting the young plants, much as you do in open ground. Place a square of cloth with its plant against the inside wall, and keep it toward the top of the planting area which will allow for some soil to settle. The leaves and plant crown extend out into light and air. Continue planting a course at a time, moistening lightly. To allow a few days between planting is further assurance of success, but place soil up to the bottom of the next row of holes to prevent the small amount used in planting drying out, which would cause the loss of the plants.

To provide light shade during the time of recovery will be wise and make for a successful venture. Use a yard square of burlap supported a foot or so above the container with sticks stuck slant-wise into the top of the soil.

We have grown vegetables in boxes (or more properly frames, since they do not have bottoms) for a number of years. At first we liked them for the order they gave the vegetable plot, but we soon learned how much easier they were to tend. We also learned how much more productive a vegetable garden grown in this manner was than one planted in the conventional manner in open ground, because the frames are handled as individual units and may be replanted as soon as the crop is harvested and the soil worked up with amendments to maintain the fertility.

Let us consider the commodious boxes, their construction, location and versatility. To begin with, decide upon the size and shape to fit into your spaces, but keep in mind your arm's-length reach for a picking and care guide. A rectangular shape of four feet wide and six to eight feet long and a foot deep is adequate for an amount and variety of vegetables that can be used before the homegrown gourmet deliciousness begins to wane. On hillsides these frames may be used to create level beds like small terraces (see illustrations on page 167 for construction details).

This mode of gardening is an outstanding way to conserve soil and water. Where soil is unsuited to the growth of annuals—either flower or vegetable—the containers may be filled economically with a soil formula to meet the needs of individual plant varieties. Either vegetables or flowering

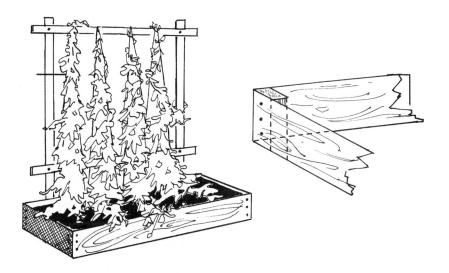

A garden box or frame about 4 x 8 feet and a foot deep is a good size and will accommodate three rows of plants. If one side is along a path, climbing beans or peas will require the least ground area. Make the box of rot-retardant wood—redwood, cedar or cypress. By giving soft wood such as pine two coats of asphalt emulsion, even pine will last for a decade. Construction details are shown for the corners. To strengthen the box use 2 x 3 inch wood, and nail in place with large galvanized nails.

Climbing string beans produce abundantly when grown in commodious 2 x 2 x 2 foot boxes. This bed of four hills yielded 6½ pounds.

Square, three-tier strawberry pyramid. May be made on only 5 square feet of ground area. If space is limited a two-tier pyramid may be made with a 4-foot base, as this one was.

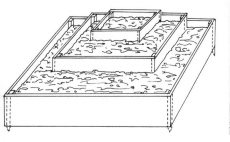

plants will grow with a normal soil (pH 7) except asparagus, which needs a bit more alkaline, and also because of its root spread and character is better suited to open ground growing. Wooden tubs and large clay pots are ideal for plants not grown in large numbers like conventional row crops, and may include eggplant, cucumbers, the cut-and-grow-again leaf vegetables and the ever-popular small-fruited tomato plants that thrive in a minimum sixteen-inch wood tub. Rhubarb also grows well in tubs and is colorful and delicious.

Locate your vegetable growing area in as much sun as you have. Adverse factors that affect the thrifty growth and maturity of plants may be compensated for to some extent with light but more frequent feeding. Careful choice of kinds and varieties also can mean success under what might be classed as unfavorable situations by plant scientists.

Although vegetables are rated to need full sun which is considered six hours each day, many kinds will grow with exposures that might be called half shade and those that grow in full sun through winter months may mature rapidly in summer with very little sun due to reflected light from the sky. Also kinds that become table-ready quickly will be successful under less than ideal conditions. The midget vegetables developed for severe climates with short growing seasons may hold the answer to problems encountered in the ever-lessening land areas. These delightful plants will be discussed later in detail. We are often surprised at the good report plants turn in. The will to survive seems inherent in most of nature's creatures. Three or four such boxes will allow for rotation of plants for soil health. A rotation guide is shown in chapter 2. Frequent replanting with varieties more suited to the advancing season will ensure quicker maturity, better quality and less insect damage. One example is leaf lettuce through the warm months.

Paths may be laid with plastic sheeting and covered with small gravel to provide weed and mud-free walking surfaces, but if the garden is to be tended and enjoyed by wheelchair persons the paths will, or course, need to be wide enough for easy access and of wood or other material easy to wheel over. This kind of garden is especially suited to those persons —the elevation brings the working surface within easy reach.

A quonset vegetable protection frame is insurance against depredations of most wildlife.

In areas where gophers and moles are present, inch-mesh galvanized chicken netting fastened onto the bottom before the frames are set will protect the crops from these intruders. If excessive seepage comes through the garden, plastic bottoms will ensure controlled year-round moisture.

A quonset-shaped frame of $^1/_2$-inch mesh hardware cloth is practical for a space about four feet by four feet and will not require reinforcement if the ends are made from the same material. These may be fastened to the bowed frame of the quonset with short pieces of pliable rubber-covered wire that will be easy to undo for crop tending and harvest.

This large frame may be converted to a coldframe with opaque plastic covering to start frost-tender summer vegetables earlier than may be done in the open unprotected garden. A muslin cover will give gentle forcing for early cucumbers and bush-type summer squash.

Smaller quonset-shaped coverings may be contrived to protect row seedlings from too much sun or wildlife by using wire coat hangers for supports. Clip off the hook and twisted wire, form the remaining wire into a half-circle, stick the ends into the soil and drape with discarded nylon window screening to give just the right amount of shade for summer seedlings.

Set up a priority for things to grow. Consider the ease of starting plants in pots and other containers. My favorite is a carefree egg carton for small numbers of seed-plants and particularily hard-to-germinate beets, chard and spinach. Fill the egg cups with potting soil, moisten thoroughly, and place two or three seeds in each section in shallow holes made with a pencil or pot label. Then close the carton and label and date each container so you will know when to expect the small plants to appear, and when they will need strong light to prevent damping off. Few seeds require light to sprout, so there will seldom be need to water until the young seedlings appear—about four days for lettuce, a week for chard and spinach. Because seeds have different germinating (sprouting) times it is not wise to plant more than one kind in a container. Small containers remove the temptation to mix different varieties.

Seed size is a clue to the ease of growth. Large seeds like radishes, turnips and mustard produce plants that do not need much pampering and are ideal if garden time is limited or if you are new at the garden game. Buy difficult-to-start tomato, eggplant and pepper plants. Keep in season with varieties and don't overplant!

Transplant (prick off) the seedlings when true leaves (second set) appear into small pots or space at least three inches apart in seed flats to allow room to grow to open-garden size or into larger pots for house plants. This transplanting phase is important, because few plants are strong enough to withstand the rigors of open ground, or have roots enough to grow in pots of considerable size, without the right kind of soil.

When seedlings are moved to open garden, tender plants like eggplant, peppers and tomatoes may be protected from cold by plastic water bottles (remove the bottoms and caps) until the right temperature comes for full night exposure. Another protective device for hardy plants are plastic berry baskets, or for larger plants a device can be made from window screening after the design shown in chapter 3.

Peas, beets, beans and carrots grow was a good old-time ditty, but doesn't fit in a year-round garden climate when March is too late to plant peas, too early for beans or corn, but ideal for most root crops, which if planted at once will be ready to harvest before the heat of summer comes.

Freeze your surplus of vegetables or fruits for delightful and delicious out-of season feasting. Make loose-packs by freezing on trays before packaging, so that any quantity may be used at a time. Ask your county home adviser for leaflets on the best kinds and ways to preserve your gourmet surplus. This data will also be a guide to varieties to plant for best freezing quality, which are likewise best for fresh eating.

In the midget vegetable line 'Midget Hybrid' sweet corn is ideal for fresh eating and with the slimmest cob takes less room in the freezer.

We are most enthusiastic about these diminutive plants; the produce is delicious, and because they are small-structured (dwarf), they bear sooner and you may have a complete garden from corn to watermelons in an area you would normally devote to one of those alone.

Midget vegetables are made to order with the small-scale farmer in mind, whether indoors or outside, but unlike dwarf fruit trees that produce full-size delicious fruits, these diminutive plants bear almost individual or two-serving size eggplant, several kinds of peppers and tomatoes, cantaloupe and watermelons through summer. Leaf and root vegetables may grow year-round, cabbage and head lettuce during the cool months. Park Seed Company, Greenwood, S. C. 29647, has a special collection of these small-scale vegetable seeds.

Planting in containers—indoors

Most vegetables and herbs can be grown indoors and thereby go from seed packet to salad bowl and cooking pot. But why indoors? For out-of-season food, for house decoration and for an interesting hobby that does not demand excessive exertion. Pot gardening offers a stimulating avocation for wheelchair persons and others confined indoors; in addition are the rewards of tasty vegetables and the freshness plants bring into the house. The companionship with green things growing gives one's spirit an uplift not easily found in other pursuits.

One can find space all over the house—on window sills, shelves, hanging baskets, bedside tables, terraces and balconies. One can begin anytime, but indoor gardening is especially valuable during winter in cold areas, and all year where there may not be outdoor space.

Concentrate on kinds that reach table-ready size quickly and continue to grow for a considerable time like the decorative cut-and-grow-again leafy vegetables which are delicious to eat, pleasing to smell and beautiful to look upon. These include red and green chard, leaf lettuce in various kinds and colors, mustard, endive, spinach, and curly cress. All of the above will grow with medium light. Varieties that normally grow through the summer, however, will require stronger light and warmth.

Not all root vegetables are feasible to grow in pots, but radishes and 'Little Finger' carrots (Burpee Seed) are best for pots, while 'Tiny Sweet' carrots that are round like radishes are better suited to open ground cultivation. These are in the midget vegetable collection offered by Park Seed Company. Each of these will mature in about two months. When carrots begin to form roots, plant another pot or box for continuous supply. Visitors may mistake the lacy carrot tops for an exotic fern or eggplant blossoms for a rare summer-flowering plant, and peppers will add a colorful touch to a summer picnic table.

How many of a kind should you plant? This will depend not only on your space, but the amount you can use before the plant begins to toughen. It is better to keep young plants coming on than to plant every pot at one time. A rule of thumb that doesn't always work out in practice is: when harvest begins, replant, but not necessarily the same variety because some kinds do better at one time of year than another.

But back to how many to plant. This depends somewhat upon the number in the family, but for two people, four chard plants is ample. An eight-inch pot or two of carrots and one of radishes will give you an idea of what to expect.

If you have outdoor garden space but live where winters come in dark and cold to last for several months, your houseplant vegetable garden will in all likelihood be confined to the cold months. Apartment people may enjoy their vegetable garden year-round. However, no matter where you live, the emphasis on plant material should shift from winter-hardy kinds to those that grow best with more warmth. With the changing season different kinds and varieties will thrive and provide stimulating activity as well as a change in menu makings.

How to begin, and what to grow, and how to harvest and use your vegetables and herbs is of concern to every grower. Take into account temperature and humidity requirements of plants. Both may be altered and improved to some extent by using one's imagination, suggestions offered here and proven methods. You may want and need to augment the existing light to provide greater growing opportunities as the need is proven and circumstances allow. The least expensive gro-lamps are portable fluorescent lights which make it possible to grow sturdy plants in an otherwise impossible situation. New seedlings for the coming season's garden will add a note of spring to your rooms. Most seed catalogs offer quite sophisticated and colorful plant-starting devices and some greenhouse people are making easy-to-attach window units that turn any window into a beautiful year-long garden.

Choose the kinds of containers to meet the needs of your plants. Root crops do not need the depth of soil if those kinds mentioned above are chosen carefully. Leaf lettuce that comes to table-ready size rapidly will not need root depth but the cut-and-grow-again chard should have a deeper pot.

Set all pots on beds of charcoal or gravel in pans or saucers to allow for excess moisture to seep away without ruining the shelf they occupy. This reservoir of moisture will also aid in supplying humidity to both the plants and the house atmosphere.

To dress up either plastic or common clay pots decorative cachepots are not expensive and will last for years.

Lightweight synthetic soil elements provide a carefree growth medium that may make it possible for a number of pots and baskets to safely occupy a shelf which the heavier weight of conventional soil would break down.

Mixes composed of peat moss and vermiculite have an advantage of being disease free and may be used over again, but they should be sterilized in the kitchen oven to make sure root insects and/or diseases have not been growing along with your luxuriant kitchen garden. To do this: set your oven temperature control to 140°, then place the soil to be treated in broad shallow pans, no more than two inches deep, so that the center of the soil bulk will reach the desired temperature of 140° readily; place the pans in the oven and close the door. Maintain the temperature for exactly thirty minutes by a reliable timer. It is important to be accurate in order to preserve the beneficial organisms and destroy the harmful ones.

Next to the correct soil comes water, which is all-important in the growth of plants and may carry plant nutrients as well as moisture (for the life processes of plants). It is possible to mix a very weak plant food solution to use each time a potful of thriving plants are watered, instead of wondering when you gave a plant its vitamins, minerals and other life-sustaining food elements.

Choose a plant food to suit the needs of your kitchen garden vegetables. Leaf plants require more nitrogen while root crops will develop more satisfactorily if the nutrient solution is higher in phosphorus and potash.

These remarks about plant nutrition apply equally to ornamentals.

Another kind of indoor gardening that is more familiar includes sprouting. Investigate the literature on this subject in magazines and books. A small volume I use and have found accurate as well as fun to read is *The Beansprout Book* by Gay Courter. Another most charming book on sprouts, one attractive to the children in your family, is *The Jar Garden* by Dorothy Weeks (Woodbridge Press).

Besides the well-known bean sprouts you may venture into alfalfa and cress, which is the easiest to grow because you do not go through a daily rinsing process, but plant the seeds on moist paper toweling. Like magic you have a delightful dish of green salad plants from which you can cut a few times, and in the meantime another plate of spicy cress can be growing.

Herbs for good taste and good looks may be moved from their traditional location on kitchen window sills and grown along with other plants into more prominent locations throughout the house for display of beauty, perfume and form.

Because herb seeds are slow to germinate (sprout) and you need only a few plants of any one kind except parsley, you may want to shop for those you want in small containers and repot into four-or six-inch pots to grow to pinching size. If you are to grow your own try the egg carton for starting the seedlings. Nurseries and garden shops offer a variety of herbs and you may find some that are new to you and intriguing to try, both for their growth forms and seasoning attributes. Another way to acquire a collection of herbs is by barter with other herb growers.

Grow dill weed for height, an airy look and good taste in a variety of recipes. Chive plants can decorate and color a variety of dishes besides baked potato with cream cheese. Planted among leafy vegetables they aid in aphid control. Rosemary and sweet marjoram are for meat seasoning, basil to use in tomato dishes—either freeze or oven dry some for winter, since it is an annual. Tarragon for salad dressings is not as aggressive as it is credited to be. These are all well-behaved delightful small-to-medium size plants that may be grown compatibly together in a sort of window box container to make a varied picture of contrasting foliage, texture and growth forms. Oregano and mint, however, tend to overrun their allotted space and will hasten to fill almost any size container, so you might as well start with a six-inch pot and when it becomes overgrown (pot-bound) divide and share with an herb fancier friend.

Most herbs are warmth lovers, but parsley if given a cool location will reward you with quantities of mild-flavored garnishing greens. Parsley seeds are slow to sprout, but soaking a few hours in warm water will soften the hard shells. The seeds may be planted directly in a shallow pot (called a fern pan) to grow into a delightful potful of delicious, spicy green. Cover the pot with glass or a plastic bag to conserve moisture during the ten-day to two-week germinating period.

This is perhaps a good time to distinguish between herbs and spices. Herbs are living plants, while spices are seeds, bark, roots or other mature portions of shrubs or trees.

Pot marigold (calendula) and nasturtium are neither true herbs nor vegetables, but lend old-fashioned charm as well as color and seasonings to food. Pot marigold, long a favorite with pioneer housewives, is just as useful as ever. The petals may be used to color soups, cheese and butter as well as make a spot of sunshine on a dark day. Because these useful flowers are subject to mildew and also because they come to bloom rather quickly, keep new plants coming on. They are robust enough to plant directly into an eight-inch fern pan. Sow about ten seeds at one time and thin out as they become overgrown.

Nasturtiums are a colorful standby for summer window boxes, but will grow through winter and trail from a hanging shelf. The dwarf forms make charming pot plants and bring fragrance with the freely borne flowers, piquant leaves for salad and green fruits which contribute a distinctive taste to pickles and are a good substitute for expensive capers.

You may imagine you would not have insects on your indoor plants, but let us examine some ways these troublesome creatures may enter your green haven. You begin with sterile soil—peat moss and vermiculite—but if it is reused infestations from root crops and other means may occur, or they may be brought in by plants you purchase from local nurseries. How to sterilize the soil has been written up earlier in this chapter.

If you bring in plants other than those you grow from seed, examine the new plants carefully. Market vegetables are possible carriers of aphids and thrips. Unsterilized pots and containers may harbor insects. Wash after each use in a cleansing medium like Clorox and plenty of clean water.

Flying insects that enter the house are more difficult to control, because there are few areas where an occasional fly, bee, moth or other winged creature isn't present. They may also hitchhike on the coats of animals or our own shoes or clothing.

For control, you may find a complete vegetable dust easier to use than a spray, but don't overlook the ease of control with water. An inexpensive spray device that attaches to a household faucet will be easy to use and effective. Pots may be turned on their side by first covering the soil area with aluminum foil to prevent soil falling out into the sink or bathtub. This makes it possible to spray the underside of the leaves where many of the plant lice live. A dusting box may be made from a cardboard carton by removing one side (see page 27).

Pruning

Good pruning is good plant grooming. Study a plant's natural habit of growth before starting to shape it, to discover how closely it can be made to conform to your needs. Indeed, this knowledge should be a prerequisite to planting it in the garden. Knowing a plant's growth form assures that it will be just right in the garden. Only by knowing when it will flower and/or fruit can you use other plants with it to glorify the landscape.

The basic theory of pruning is: if you want branching, cut to a leaf node, where a bud will be found. The outer buds, those nearest the end of a stem, will be first to send forth branches because they are younger and more vigorous than those further down the branch. By tying the limb into an arch many of the buds will break at once. Nature does this to perfection along the gracefully curving canes of climbing roses and plants with similar habits of growth.

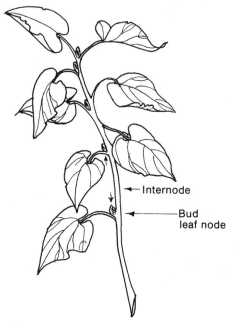

This tendency of buds to break into branches is taken advantage of when growing a full and beautiful hedge. Plants that do not break freely are not suited to hedge form. Other nonflowering plants are pruned to produce more luxuriant foliage and to acquire the shape desired in the garden.

Timely pruning can prevent expensive repairs later on. First, consider the growth pattern of individual trees. If they are globe- or vase-shaped, don't try to make a columnar form.

To maintain the size of a tree and lessen the canopy of leaves, cut to a branch, which does not encourage the abundance of new growth that cutting to a bud does. It is used in the development and particularily in the maintenance of ornamental trees. Any tree may on occasion require thinning, because we never know when a dormant bud may develop into branches and require removal. The two general goals of pruning are for shape (to secure the correct number of branches) and to encourage bud development for production of leaves, flowers and fruit.

Cutting flowers and clipping spent stems may be called mild pruning and if carefully done there will be less pruning to do in the garden during the dormant season. Pay particular attention to cutting roses and nipping off fading flowers. This is explained in detail later in this chapter. *Think* before you clip! Always cut to a leaf node. Successive flowering of both annuals and perennials is missed by not shearing the plants sharply as soon as the flowers begin to fade. This is especially true of small plants that edge paths.

Evergreen plants may be pruned at any time without serious bleeding, but it is unwise to prune them late in autumn, because a warm spell could encourage new growth that might be frosted. Deciduous plants are pruned while the leaves are off. That is, the heavy pruning is done then, because when they are resting, or dormant, the sap is not flowing and they should not bleed to any extent. Also, when bare of leaves the entire tree may be analyzed. I favor waiting to shorten smaller branches that are to remain as part of the permanent plant until closer to spring where late frosts are likely to occur.

How does one know which plants to prune in winter and which ones to prune later? Consider their time of bloom. The gayest spring-flowering shrubs—spirea, bridal wreath, forsythia, syringa and flowering quince (*Japonica*)—represent those that are pruned either during or immediately following bloom, because they flower on mature or at least year-old wood.

Summer-flowering deciduous shrubs and trees are pruned when the other dormant pruning is done because they bloom on the current season's wood. Crape myrtle and *Buddleia* (summer lilac) are two familiar examples. Consider further whether flowering plants' lavish bloom develops into a brilliant show of fruit for later enjoyment, or if the flowers are the main display or if they give a bonus of colorful autumn leaves.

The deciduous group also includes trees and vines. Roses may be either deciduous or evergreen depending upon the temperature zone, but are treated as deciduous in the pruning program. That is, the heavy pruning is done in late winter.

Remove dead or diseased branches as soon as they are discovered. Broken branches should be pruned off carefully. How far back they will need to be cut will depend upon where the limb has been broken, and if the break is square or splintered. Sometimes the branch must be removed entirely. Likewise, interfering branches develop in almost any plant during the time of rapid growth. If the interfering branch is needed in the structure of the plant it may be trained and spaced by means of a brace formed of withes—pieces of twigs twisted together, which are more satisfactory than a brace made of thin wood with a half-scallop in each end (see chapter 1).

To understand pruning techniques consider the way plants grow. It is important to know that very few trees grow upward along the trunks. That is, the tree does not lengthen from the ground, but from the buds. This is why as long as the terminal buds of branches are alive the plant continues to grow taller, wider or longer, in case of vines. If the terminal bud is destroyed in some way, choose a branch that can be guided upward to form a new trunk. This is frequently done with *Cedrus deodara* and other evergreens to develop a more compact tree.

Good pruning builds strength. Prune to a branch rather than stubbing off major limbs in the middle of nowhere, which often results either in a proliferation of twiggy, useless branches or dieback of the entire limb stub. This condition is often seen in wild woodlands.

Learn to recognize good pruning. For example, each crotch of sizable branches is a scaffold or shoulder that strengthens the limbs; healing will take place only at those points. Use large enough limbs for balance. Don't prune to little boughs. To keep the tree in balance, don't remove a large limb on one side of the tree without equaling the branch load on the opposite side. Work for rhythmic flowing lines.

Armchair pruning, that is reading without applying the directions, is not the way to learn. Don't read directions one day and try to apply them the next. Wisdom and observation is necessary if one is to become a good pruner. While gaining wisdom, try to use caution when pruning. It is better to err by the too-little use of tools, than to get carried away and end up with a mutilated tree.

When you have studied and practiced pruning so that you can go into your garden and prune with assurance, you will have acquired one of the most satisfying skills of gardening. To me, there is nothing that gives the promise of a bountiful harvest of flowers and fruit so surely as the correct pruning of permanent plants. Much of this skill comes through observation in your own garden. Notice what the former season's pruning produced, how it could have been done better or at least differently and have the fortitude to remedy mistakes as soon as possible and the determination not to make the same ones again.

Pruning, like any other garden chore, requires proper tools. You will need two sizes of shears (clippers) and eighteen- to twenty-four-inch loppers. I've used and recommended a lopper with an eighteen-inch handle for years. It is strong and yet light enough for a woman or weekend gardener. When branches get too big for this size shear, the saw will be easier to use. A regular folding curved-blade pruning saw is an absolute must for gardens more than two years old (see the section on tools and equipment in chapter 5).

Pare the ragged bark of saw cuts smooth with a sharp knife so the pruning compound will make a tighter seal which will prevent borers and disease from entering the wound. It is good first aid to first shellac the cambium cells (the smooth moist inner bark) before applying the pruning paste, which may be caustic to the delicate cells that grow out and heal the wound. Take the shellac and paste (an asphalt base product) into the garden with you and apply to cuts as soon as pruning of a plant is finished. By painting as you go, the change in work will rest you, and you won't finish too late to do the sealing. It is important to apply this product to fresh cuts, as it binds best on a moist surface.

Thumbnail pruning (pinching) can be practiced on tender growing shoots. Nipping off the ends or tips of the branches will slow down the rapid seasonal growth and encourage branching during the active growing period, to the extent that the scaffold is begun earlier and wasted energy lessened.

Woody vines like grapes and climbing roses continue to lengthen or grow from their tips. Observe that when the tip, which carries the terminal bud, is broken off, branches will grow from several leaf nodes along the stem. It is at these nodes that the buds are located. These cells are specialized and may become flowering, fruiting stems or new wood growth, depending upon their characteristic forms.

From this, we can readily see that if branching is wanted, we shorten back the plant to conform to the gardening plan. If a tree is allowed to grow without any direction, its shape will be influenced by the environment: prevailing wind, the amount of light the plant gets and its closeness to other objects, particularly buildings or solid walls. It is far better to remove branches that are not to be part of the permanent framework when they are small or young than to allow them to remain for even a season, because small cuts heal readily but large ones take several months and even years to heal.

Maximum production and fulfillment of flowering plants can be enjoyed only through proper pruning. Roses, for example, can be encouraged to bloom all season long if they are intelligently pruned, and the flowers kept cut. It is because roses bloom on current-season (new) wood growth that it is possible to enjoy a continuing crop of flowers from early summer through autumn.

Learning to prune roses is like learning any other pruning technique. We need theory, but we need practical experience as well. Bush roses and tree forms are pruned in the same manner. Disregard the fact that the flowering head of the tree rose is atop a tall thin naked stalk.

The pruning of hybid tea roses and/or the grandiflora class are very much the same. Prune heavily in late winter or early spring. Remove half to two-thirds of the past year's growth. Retain as many as five stout canes if that number can be spaced without crowding; otherwise, select and keep the number that are available. Until the dormant buds of older canes begin to swell and show pink, it is difficult for a novice gardener to find them, but look for them just above a leaf scar. This newly pruned bush will form the frame you will work with during summer, although in older plants it is often possible to saw out some of the old wood during summer as it is replaced by new, vigorous growth from the bud union.

When canes are cut out, do so smooth with the crown. Never leave a stub to decay.

Because floribunda types are pruned more lightly to conform to their more delicate structure, we generally cut to the first or second plump bud below the flower cluster. Cane selection may be necessary after the second or third year in the garden. This is particularily true of some strong-growing plants. These generous bloomers are excellent to use for drapery over structures or walls, or to form a three-foot edging or small hedge around a patio.

When pruning climbers, practice cutting back the seasonal-flowering short stems that emerge from the buds along the canes, as was discussed earlier. After these stems have produced a second bloom, that portion of the plant should be removed. If this is faithfully practiced, you will not have an overgrown garden.

Generally, the only flowers produced the first year on climbing roses of the hybrid tea class will be a few from the short wood that made the plant when purchased. The short climber, pillar, roses frequently produce flowers from annual stems. 'High Noon' is an excellent example of a western pillar rose.

After the third year begin cutting out the older canes, or at least remove the outer portion that has bloomed, either entirely or down to robust buds, or where the cane may already have branched and put forth a new cane.

Considering the different classes of roses, the hybrid tea outsells, outblooms and outgrows all other kinds. Until recently the floribunda had few fans, but with new introductions and the vogue of planters and pots of flowering plants for patios and outdoor living areas, this delightful little many-flowered bush is gaining its justly deserved popularity.

For formal effect nothing can equal the regal tree roses but to cover walls, banks and even buildings, the type called climbers is unrivaled. Roses, as we can see from this brief listing of types, can really make a garden. 'Silver Moon" will cover a pergola or arbor with a lovely flowering crown. 'Mermaid' will make a beautiful glossy green impenetrable hedge, or a foot-high ground cover. 'Gold of Ophir' or the delicately flowered thornless yellow *banksiae* will grow to the top of very tall trees, but because they are not twining, as are the wild grape and poison oak or ivy, they will not cause damage to the trees.

Production from plants of any variety depends upon the way they are pruned and shaped, the kind and amount of nutrients used, and the kind of spray and when and how it is applied. Learn to prune with a purpose. Don't just go out and whack away. Study each plant's growth and fruiting habits. Field demonstrations may be given by city and county parks, local tree-growing firms, nurseries, garden clubs or adult education classes. Watch the local press for information and make it a point to attend some of these for visual instruction.

Most state agricultural colleges and the United States Department of Agriculture have excellent booklets that demonstrate the technique of pruning and care of trees around the home. Many of these may also be had from your local county farm adviser, who may have lists of varieties and spray schedules for your area.

These ambassadors of the universities have at their fingertips professionally written pamphlets on almost every phase of garden management, and they cost no more than a friendly visit to their office.

Getting plants ready for winter

By the time winter comes it is often too late to do very much about protecting plants against frost damage; yet this is one of the important seasonal routines and should not be neglected no matter where you live and garden.

To prevent frost damage is the only sensible way out, but how to forestall such a natural force needs some discussion. One course is to plant those things which are not damaged by cold, but how do you know which plants those are? Many catalogs that list tender plants are careful to give accurate temperature tolerances. Observations of plants in your neighborhood will be helpful.

How much protection a plant will need depends upon several factors: the inherent hardiness, and its state of growth when winter sets in; the location in the garden and the severity of the season beyond the normal temperatures expected; whether it is a wet or dry winter; and how continuous the cold is when it shuts down.

The question of tender plants' hardiness arises anywhere in regions where various degrees of temperature are common, such as are found at the northerly or colder areas of a zone. It is often better to use the temperature rating of the next coldest area, remembering that altitude also affects temperature. Broken land masses often create thermal (relatively frost-free) belts that may be surrounded by land with several months of nightly killing frost.

By setting out tender plants after warm weather arrives, you can allow a full season of growth in the garden, in which wood cells mature, or harden up, naturally and are ready for winter. If borderline plants are set out in the fall, however, they may break into rapid new growth as a result of the roots being placed in fresh nourishing soil after the confinement of the container, and be killed by even slight frost.

Jack Frost's art may be amusing on a windowpane, but it can play havoc in the garden. The first killing frost may occur in cold islands, at higher elevations and in regions away from coastal plains, following rain in late autumn. Frost warnings are a part of nightly weather forecasts during the months when protection of tender plants is necessary. Listen and act; make your own weather map before the nightly fruit-frost broadcast. Go out into a dark place and look at the stars; if they are twinkling brightly, cold blue in color, chances are there will be a heavy frost or at least below-freezing temperatures recorded. The two are not synonymous. Frost depends upon the dewpoint, which in simple terms means the temperature at which moisture from the atmosphere collects. If the humidity conditions are favorable for dew to form before 32°F., there will be white frost; otherwise, it can get down very low without the presence of ice on plants. This is known as black frost; often more devastating than ice covering.

Good gardening practices prevent frost damage to plants in several ways. For example, harden plant tissues by spacing irrigations further apart, but do not allow them to dry out. As wood cells mature less water will be needed. This is a technique that requires timing and experience, but is an important phase of growing semitender plants. Also, you can withhold late applications of high-nitrogen fertilizer so plant tissues will mature; and make a careful choice of plants to withstand your average low temperature. Do not prune tender shrubs and perennials like fuchsias, geraniums or lantana until late March. Plants' foliage provides warmth that aids in frost resistance. Mounding soil about their crowns also helps protect vital areas, and even if the branches are frosted the root may be kept alive. The crowns of herbaceous plants that die to the ground each season may be easily protected with earth or heeled in cold frames for the somber short days.

Earth mounds about newly planted citrus and avocado trees will lessen frost damage to the bud union. The same technique will carry roses through a severe winter. The mounds must be taken away before spring growth begins, otherwise the joining of root and fruit wood may send up sprouts and kill the flowering plant.

Shelter plants in containers that are too large to move easily with a sheath of straw held in place with wire netting. In regions where rain sometimes replaces snow, cover with plastic or other waterproof material during storms.

Corn stalks make good insulated sheaths for trees. Work them in close to the tree stem among the branches, so as not to shut light away from the leaves. Bind loosely with strong cord. Gather long grasses—tule or bamboo may generally be had for the cutting. An excursion to a wild planting area for these can be an occasion for an unusual, long-remembered outing for the whole family.

A thick mulch of large leaves that more or less form a thatch over plants, when held in place by evergreen boughs or wire netting, will protect plants even as tender as fuchsias from freezing where temperatures do not go below 20° F. A bit of mouse bait tossed into the crown of plants before bedding down is good insurance. I like to use inverted bushel baskets when available to cover the leaves, as winter overcoats for the tenderest plants. It is not a bad idea, on a nice day when the snow is off for a time, to turn up the thatch and examine the plants for mice nests, mole runs or gopher damage. Shelter will be appreciated by the vegetable and animal kingdom in like manner. All materials should be ready to use at a moment's notice.

Frost protection where winter snows are replaced by rain requires the utmost ingenuity, and more plants may be lost from frost in warm zones than in colder regions, because they continue to grow throughout the winter. Bedding down as is done in cold climates is not practicable. A warm spell may start new growth, and rains will soak through almost any covering and cause severe ice damage when the temperature falls to freezing. Where periods of growth are interrupted with freezing temperatures, generally following a rain, the plant is abnormally full of moisture and the soggy soil freezes about the plant's crown, causing the bark to split.

One way to lessen frost damage in the open garden is to go out about the time the thermometer begins to mount and quickly wash down the garden. This will remove the ice from foliage and lessen the damage tremendously; this is especially effective on leaf vegetables. In order to do this, hoses must be drained the day before, since on a really cold morning ice may remain in a hose until noon. Try to remember to disconnect the hose and drain it as soon as you are through with this defrosting operation, because then you are sure it is done. In areas where the need for irrigation of the open garden is past, washing off of frost may be the principal use for hoses. However, cold frames and potted plants may need moistening. Draining hoses saves on repair bills, and since a mended hose is never as strong as before damage occurs, this extra precaution saves time, money and worry.

Some of the following practical ideas may save many valuable plants. When covering plants with cloth, always place several stakes about the plant for the cloth to rest upon, above and away from the plant's leaves. Because dew falling early in the evening will wet the cloth, if it is in contact with the foliage, it will freeze hard to the plant, causing more damage than if it were unsheltered. Paper cartons make wonderful plant protectors. They offer good insulation, are quickly set over plants, and if different sizes are collected, they may be nested when removed during the day, making storage easier. They need no tying down or stakes to prevent frost-wetted material from touching and burning leaves. Although they will be ruined by rain, more can be had from the corner grocery. (Because it seldom freezes when raining, covering at that time is not necessary, but it may be expecting too much for a gardener to be that careful.)

A lighted lantern or electric light placed under a canvas cover will give some protection while the plant is small, but if it isn't going to be hardy to your average low temperatures when older, I'd strongly advise against planting it in the first place. Don't gamble more than a few degrees on a plant standing the cold of an area. I like to have the leeway in my favor. It seems such needless waste for plants to be frozen to death.

However, to some gardeners, even elaborate frost protection devices are worthwhile in order to enjoy an especially favorite plant. One feature not commonly used is living windscreens. Hedges occupy the least space, and through trimming grow into dense shelters, but for larger plantings windbreaks will be more effective. Foliage impedes air currents, absorbs both heat and cold while sheltering plants, and may modify the temperature by several degrees, thereby providing enough protection for hardy plants to survive.

Locate the windscreens correctly in relation to prevailing winds and what they are designed to shelter. This forethought may help you decide the best location for the garden. Unlike walls or fences of solid material, there is no swirl of air on the sheltered side of the plant windscreen, but if you choose to build a shelter instead of growing one it has been found more effective to run the boards horizontally and allow about a foot between them at the bottom, lessening the spacing as you near the top. This design acts much like a hedge as a wind filter. Another way a hedge will add to the productivity of the garden is to act as a snow trap. The melt from spring thaw will provide moisture for at least early summer.

In prairie regions windscreens are almost indispensable to protect fruit and leaf buds from spring cold and trees from mechanical injury. The texture and density of the foliage mass is a determining factor in the protection it will provide. Leafy plantings may make the difference between a satisfactory garden and a disappointing failure.

Strawberry buds form in September and October, so in areas of winter snows it is important to mulch early to protect the blossom buds. Either straw or hay will guard against winter kill. Where strong winds prevail it may be advisable to hold the mulch in place with large-mesh wire or evergreen boughs. You can grow a more productive garden and more kinds of fruit (even in the northeastern tier of states) by careful selection of varieties. An advantage of vining plants is they may be taken off the trellis or support and covered with insulation material for winter. Strawberries are candidates for cold climates as well as subtropical, and because they are ground-hugging plants they present no problem with winter cover.

Finally, if the expected low winter temperature is overcoat-muffler cold, few tender plants will survive unless they are grown in a greenhouse or stored in a coldframe, and then the problem of them outgrowing the allotted space arises. Established plants resent being disturbed. Under such circumstances the tender plants should be grown in containers which can be moved under shelter without interfering with their root systems.

There is choice plant material that is hardy to each region, and we should be courageous enough to seek out that which we may grow without so much risk and catering and enjoy the winter for what it brings, remembering spring is not far behind.

Insect and rodent control

Stem and leaf

Don't think of insect control merely in terms of insecticides. This is an important means but there are others, such as outwitting and sanitation. Each method is effective for control and maximum production of flowers, fruits and vegetables.

It is a good idea to make a master plan of your plantings. List the crops you plan to grow and the damage usually caused by insects together with ways of outwitting them.

No phase of gardening is more complicated or confusing to average gardeners than insect control, and none more important. With dozens of bottles at the garden supply store, how is one to know which to buy? Study the chart on page 197 and discover three bottles of magic that show how few you will really need. Then forget about the shelf of bottles for a little while and get acquainted with the insects you are likely to meet in your garden.

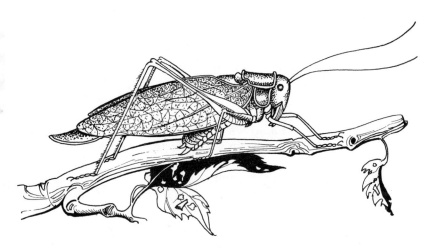

Grasshoppers are among the big chewers that are with us especially during summer, but in warm areas may be found all year.

Reading about garden insects and diseases can be quite discouraging, unless you keep a sense of proportion about the garden's uninvited guests and remember that no one plot of ground has more than a fraction of those cataloged in an encyclopedia. Also, insects are somewhat seasonal; even local bugs do not all come at one time.

Learn the different feeding habits of chewing and sucking insects for positive recognition and control. In other words, being a bug detective is an effective springboard to simplified, intelligent control. Take a bird's-eye view of the commonest garden foe, the plant-sucking aphid. Here is truly a gourmet with a universal appetite for plants. Aphids come in almost every color from delicate green to brilliant red and purple. They are favored by another common garden enemy, the ant. Where you find one you will find the other. Aphids exude a honey-sweet residue that ants find most delicious. To ensure a well-distributed and full larder they actually move aphids from one plant to another. Sucking insects do not destroy plants, but pump the juices out of leaves and young tender twigs with feeding tubes, distorting and stunting the plant's growth.

Chewing insects eat portions of leaves, or entire young seedlings. Now to detect the bugs, find out how they feed and where they live between meals. What are chewing insects' feeding habits? Snails and slugs are identical, except slugs suffer from a housing shortage; lacking true mouth parts, they slither onto a beautiful, lush, tasty leaf and go to work with sandpaper-like tongues. When they have worn the leaf through, they move to a fresh spot and begin all over again. Beetles scallop the edges of firmer leaves and tunnel into rose and camellia buds. Most caterpillar types (like measuring worms) feed as they hitch themselves along the surface of a leaf, back and forth, until there's nothing left or their hunger is gratified. Grasshoppers just tear off pieces of the leaves. Chewing creatures are most active during the cool of the day; on cloudy days they may feed continuously. So that is a good time to go through the garden and see just what is eating which.

Scale insects' feeding habits class them as sucking insects. They are divided into two groups: soft-bodied and so-called armored or shelled scale. Soft-bodied kinds are appropriately named cottony-cushion and mealybug from their downy covering. They are difficult to control with sprays until this protective covering is broken by a strong force of water from the garden hose. Shelled scale are controlled with an oil emulsion spray. Fortunately both kinds have predators. Control ant traffic up plant stems with chlordane-impregnated cotton bands fastened around the main trunk of trees, shrubs and vines to make control of scale easier and more positive.

To make the cotton bands take a length of absorbent cotton 3 inches wide and long enough to go around the tree or its branches. After the ant control material is applied fold the cotton, and apply to the plant, fold side up. Tie with two strings to prevent slipping down.

Nearly all insects have their natural enemies, and the balance of nature tends to keep the bad bugs in check. We may see ladybugs (ladybird beetles) and their larvae (young) at work in the garden. They have a ravenous appetite, but to enjoy their help we must be careful about a choice of sprays. Curtail the use of chemical sprays by using natural means and common sense. Nowhere in the garden is the stress on organic materials more important. On the chart I've listed only organic contact and stomach poison sprays. If these are used wisely these insects can be controlled and the natural beneficial predators protected.

Be sure of your method before you are sorry. Until you are sure, rely upon garden sanitation and a strong spray of water. Remove from the garden, where possible, sources of infestation; weeds are often hosts to both insects and fungi. Encourage insect-devouring lizards, toads, frogs, harmless snakes and birds by providing nest boxes, feeding trays and watering devices.

So far we have not discussed fungi and their mode of living in and on plants. Mildew and rust are the ordinary fungi of the garden and curly leaf of peach foliage and brown spot (or rot) of apricots are common in the orchard. Mildew grows on the top surface of leaves and rose buds as a downy covering. Rust, in dots like freckles, is found under the leaves and is more difficult to reach with average devices.

Neither aphids nor grasshoppers can be prevented from coming to board in your garden, but fungi can be. Learn to recognize and prevent, as far as possible, conditions under which fungi thrive. If you know the plants that are most susceptible and how fungi grow upon plants, then you can undertake prevention.

Fungi are really minute plants. They alight on moist foliage at night and if not rinsed off early in the morning before their specialized roots get hold, they actually grow on leaves. One of the best ways of controlling fungi is to give the garden a quick rinse each morning. This swish is not to be confused with watering the garden, but will dislodge fungi spores and loads of aphids, too, and may bring out of hiding worms and snails that mistake this for an early morning shower. Those big fellows may then be hand picked. Not wearing gloves can lead to a squeamish attitude toward this operation.

Since fungi cannot readily adhere to dry foliage, sprinkle early enough in the day so that plants have time to dry off before nightfall. Keep rose bushes and other host plants open for air circulation with seasonal pruning. If possible plant highly susceptible plants in the breezy area of the garden. Replacing annual plants at least once during the growing season will go a long way toward solving the mildew problem and can result in higher production.

Prevention and/or outwitting most insects may be accomplished by planting varieties that do best in a particular season when they grow quickly and so avoid serious damage.

Timing is of the greatest importance in gardening. Getting at pests while young, even in the egg stage, and before they have made serious inroads on the garden is of utmost urgency.

Decide ahead of time what means you are going to employ. Two types are available: dusts and sprays. Sprays are less expensive, but dusts are easier to use, especially with handy applicator containers. Both are effective, but you will need to find the one you like best and that does a job for you. Any control program adopted should be possible to carry out easily. Don't make it so complex that you can't find time to do it.

It is good practice to wash down the garden prior to using an insecticide in any event, because clean foliage makes a more effective base for spray than dusty leaves or those that may be coated with residues from former spray applications.

Few sprays are effective after three or four days, so the interval to spray for best control may be a week or ten days, or as far apart as a month in some cases. Plants can function much better with clean leaves, and many summer insects, notably red spider mites, are substantially controlled by sprinkling, so the garden hose is one of the most effective, easy and inexpensive ways to clean up the garden.

The aesthetic side of sprinkling the garden is pure delight, and we get a bonus besides seeing and hearing the refreshing spray; bushtits come to bathe in the spray, and using small twigs to perch upon, find aphids and other small insects and make a lunch at the same time. I have fun watering the garden with a fine spray whenever aphids appear, and a busy flock of whispering tits oblige by eating the fat plant lice. Charming insect control!

Earth-inhabiting insects

Insect and fungi that infect the plant above ground are easy to check on, but more watchful analysis is needed to detect those that attack the roots. The first warning of soil-borne insects may be ants mounding dirt in the crowns of strawberry and other plants. Root aphids and ground mealybug are two important foes. For control, dilute chlordane according to instructions and pour a half-cupful into the plant crowns. Be sure the soil is moist when using this treatment.

One of the most difficult earth inhabitants to control is the wooly apple aphid, because of its complicated life cycle. These pernacious insects damage not only their namesake plant, but allied plants as well; pyracantha is especially vulnerable.

Nematodes are quite a different organism. These and other soil miseries may be controlled with soil fumigant. Because ants do not feed on nematodes, detection is more difficult. A wan anemic look may indicate nematodes or other earth insects and/or diseases. Nematodes may be overcome to some extent by planting flowers and vegetables resistant to them or that grow in spite of them; by rotating plants in the annual garden; and by using legumes and grains such as sweet corn extensively. They are especially injurious to lettuce, carrots, beets, potatoes and other solanum plants. Don't mistake their wart-like injuries for beneficial nitrogen nodules, which are contained in sack-like vessels attached to roots of all legumes.

Corklike or gummy growths near the groundline of budded trees and roses may be caused by minute bacterial organisms sometimes present in old orchard, vineyard and farm soils and in most oak leaf mold, which makes it unsafe to use for mulching deciduous fruit trees and roses. Crowngall gets its name from the area of the plant it grows on, which makes it important to keep this vulnerable union of root and fruit or flowering wood above ground.

These organisms may enter the tree body through wounds made when hoeing or by leaving stubs when pruning away shoots or suckers. Weeds growing close to the tree should be pulled and do not leave stubs when pruning. Carefully remove some soil from around the plant so the entire sprout may be cut close. Do the same when removing the galls. Cover the wound with Bordeaux powder (copper sulfate) blended with water to the consistency of thick cream. When dry, paint with tree seal or some other asphalt emulsion product.

When planting in soils that are known to be infected with nematodes, use trees with resistant root stock and either soak the root above the graft or crown in a Bordeaux solution or at least paint the crown with this material.

A great deal has been written, both favorable and controversial, about chemicals used in the fight against plant insects and diseases. The freedom they bring to home gardeners is very real.

Three bottles of magic

	Pyrethrum. Rotenone Nicotine sulfate	Copper sulfate (Bordoil as a dormant spray (*)	Oil Emulsion (*)
The element			

	Chewing, sucking insects	Mildew Rust Peach-leaf curl Brown rot (apricots)	Scale insects
What they control			

Two-way: Combine these two for summer plant infestations.

Clean-up: Use all three for cleanup in autumn/winter—the climax of insect reproduction.

* Oil emulsion is combined with copper sulfate by manufacturers to make a safe and effective dormant spray when used at dormant strength, sold under the trade name Bordoil.

Read all labels and carefully follow all instructions and cautions.

Here are some names applied to different sprays and what they mean.

Contact spray: For aphids, thrips, whitefly, leaf hoppers and other sucking insects that damage plants by puncturing them with a feeding tube, distorting leaf and stem. The insect must be wet with the spray—the only method of control

Stomach poison: For the big chewers that devour plants. Use the same element as for contact. The spray deposits a poison residue on the leaf surface, and provides control for whatever eats it. This one application does double duty. Also use snail/slug bait.

Fungicide: For fungi: mildew, mold, smut, and rust; curly-leaf of peaches, brown rot of apricots and similar diseases. The same element is used for summer and dormant sprays, but at different dilutions.

Clean-up spray: Is what the name implies. It is composed of the elements from all three of the sprays listed above and deals a multiple blow to all insects and diseases at one time. Use only *one* measure of water. Oil emulsion alone controls scale insects and most mites like red spider mite.

Regard the directions on insecticide packages as your guarantee for a cleaner, more productive garden.

Conditions that encourage insects and fungi are prevalent in almost every garden. It is my hope that after reading the material provided here you may avoid making ideal homes for the creatures that ruin gardens. Keep the labels legible! Paint them with clear varnish; or remove and number both the bottle and label and file the label under "pest control" in a garden book. Flexible aluminum labels are excellent for this. A label that cannot be read is worse than no spray at all. Finally, keep out of reach of chidren.

Rodents

The big chewers and tunnelers are harmful earth dwellers. The damage they do in the garden is not so hard to pinpoint or control as the more highly specialized and smaller kinds that are difficult to see with the unaided eye.

Learn to distinguish between the earth movements of gophers and moles. Gophers make fine pulverized hills of soil as they tunnel from plant to plant along their burrows. Carnivorous mole runs are barely subsurface and create low ridges which may be tramped shut or beat down with a shovel to protect root drying. Vegetarian field mice use these runs in search of food and find good pickings in choice bulbs and roots which the moles skirt around in search of grubs and earthworms.

In either case prompt action is called for to save plants.

Both of these subterranean creatures are destructive to plants in their characteristic ways. Gophers have a fine gourmet appetite for choice roots. Moles serve some worthwhile service by clearing out plant-eating grubs, but damage plants by unwanted soil aeration.

As the earth warms after a rain the beneficence of moisture will be manifested in many ways. Become wise to these earth movements. Small hummocks of soil may denote weed seeds germinating. Larger mounds may be pushed up by pasture mushrooms that may take us on a quest in search of these most delectable gleanings and away from the serious business of doing something about the pulverized hills of soil that can mean one thing—gophers at work.

To an observant gardener these piles of soil start a chain reaction: gophers mounding soil and choice plants disappearing. They are busy stocking their larders against winter, after an age-old urge. This destruction may be lessened by supplying poison grain for them to store. After all, gardening is an unrelenting game.

My method of catching moles may appeal to dexterous gardeners. If and when you see the ridge of soil moving, grab a shovel and flip the mole out onto the ground and quickly dispatch it with a spat from the back of the shovel. A less patient method is to soak earthworms and/or grubs in a chlordane solution and "plant" the dead bait in the runways. Moles are more difficult to trap than gophers.

If you have a young Daniel Boone in your family who may want to run a trapline, you can well pay a bounty for gopher tails. Preventing the loss of one shrub will justify the subsidy. A way to outsmart these nocturnal varmints is to line the planting holes with inch-mesh poultry netting. Herbs in our garden were on the gophers' preferred tidbit list until we devised this method of protection.

Chapter 7
Plant Nutrition

Feeding

Plants cannot thrive unless their total requirements—food, climate and moisture—are approximately in balance. They should have a look of well-being which comes only through total nutrition. Consider feeding plants in terms of nutrition, rather than a haphazard routine often used. Apply this to soil structure and chemistry, water, weather, temperature and exposure, either to sun or shade. Air is also a factor in the assimilation of nutrients by plants.

Earth feeding is of course the oldest method of feeding plants and will always be an important method. The value of the age-old practice of dressing the soil with manure cannot be minimized. Barnyard manure is a cure-all for sick soils and ailing plants. It contains the highest amount of natural vitamin B1 available in any organic plant food, which induces growth of beneficial soil bacteria necessary for luxuriant plants. Hay and grain contain the basic soil chemicals which are returned to the soil when barnyard manure is used. Enzymes are added through the process of digestion.

Nutrients in solution are available to plants immediately. Liquid manure is an inexpensive source of mineral-rich plant food. Here is how to make it.

Nearly fill a vessel with water. Five gallons is enough for a small garden. Make a bag (from coarse cloth) of manure (horse, cow, rabbit, chicken), allowing one pound to a gallon of water. Place the bag in the water, and push it down occasionally to aid in leaching and to ensure a richer brew.

Liquid manure spells food and mois-ture. Follow the simple directions given here to brew this booster-tonic for your plants.

When bubbles begin to appear on the surface, remove the manure from the tank to avoid an objectionable odor. Bottle off the stock solution and label the containers. It is ready to use when diluted with water. The color of medium-strength tea is about right for most plants.

To liquify any plant food, place two to four tablespoons (per gallon of water) of complete plant food in a pail or watering can, or one tablespoon sulfate of ammonia per gallon for straight nitrogen. The plant food is ready to use as soon as the liquid takes up the material. If the fertilizer is combined in a coa se granular carrier, it might be well to make the liquid in a pail and strain into the watering can to avoid stopping up the sprinkler head. It is important that the soil be moist when applying plant food in solution. Liquid nutrients are ideal for potted plants, because they do not add bulk.

Plant foods often go to waste in garden workrooms because of poor management. Bags may be broken and their contents spilled, or if ammonia is part of the nitrogen element, it may become rock-hard. A good rainy-day job should be to go over the various food packages and combine those with similar formulas. Camellia, azalea and rose food generally have acid-base ingredients. Two- or four-pound coffee cans make excellent, nearly airtight containers.

"Editing" plant foods will make sure you have proper growth stimulants on hand and may save you money. Paste the name of the food on the container, or enclose in the can. Also save the analysis chart that gives the contents and shows how much to use. You might do the same with nonacid-base plant foods.

Wise use of fertilizers not only produces better crops but saves money on pest control as well. The technique of application means the difference between bumper crops maturing quickly and a straggling harvest, and when the yield is produced over a shorter time, less insect and fungi control is necessary. Fungi particularly don't often damage annuals during early growth. A good rule of thumb is: don't use nitrogen after plants begin to come to bloom or make fruit or seed, unless they are season-long producers like peppers, eggplant or broccoli.

For more information on plant nutrition, see Appendixes.

Watering methods for plants in the open ground

Water is one of our national concerns. In areas of low rainfall it is necessary to supply moisture to plants between this most appreciated of nature's blessings, and generally for the dry summer months.

As in other phases of gardening which affect the health and production of plants, we need to learn how to water to get the best results. A "moisture sense" means an ability to gauge how much and when to use water and the method that best serves the plants' needs. While no amount of explaining will take the place of experience, some discussion may point the way to an understanding of what it means to irrigate plants.

There are two common watering faults—using either too little or too much. Both are equally bad, but with widely differing consequences. Too little encourages surface roots and plants wilt with the warmth of the sun. Too much drives the air from the soil, creates a sour condition, drowns the feeder roots, rots the anchor roots, and leaches plant food below the feeder root zone. Both methods defeat the purpose of applying refreshment to a parched soil and wilting plants between rains.

As for symptoms, a general look of dejection—limp foliage, lifeless branches and withering new bud growth—is about the same under both circumstances. It is only by digging into the soil that one can tell where the fault lies. In one instance the plant is starved for moisture, and in the other it is suffocated by drowning.

Here is a good way to test for moisture. Take out a shovelful of soil a little way from the plant a few hours after watering. If the moisture has penetrated only a few inches the trouble is too little, but if the soil is soggy, the water has been running too long.

Merely waving a hose over the garden is a waste of time and water. I favor sprinkling as an efficient, carefree method. On hillsides and in flower beds where one doesn't wish to make basins about each plant, or furrows (neither of which is practical because of the time required to cultivate after each soaking), sprinkling is the best method to wet the ground thoroughly. A perforated plastic hose or one made of muslin are both excellent devices for row crops, narrow parkways and similar areas. It is not easy to weave hoses in and out among flower stalks, but if enough lengths can be got together, they may be left in the beds until the plants are through blooming.

Let us now consider watering along paths and at corners. A satisfactory device for these areas and for either round or square beds is the shrub head made by Rainbird and sold as number 2400. One may get these heads to meet his own particular needs. A two-tine fork mount by the same company is easily pushed into the soil by slight pressure of the foot. It will be a convenience to have a mount for each head, and may speed watering because more than one set may be going at the same time, but the brass heads may be changed quickly.

The round and square patterns are set for sixteen feet of coverage while the one-half and one-fourth-circle heads are set for twelve and one-half feet. They may be made to water lesser areas by adjusting the water pressure but those are the maximum coverages. Another distinct advantage of these sprinkler devices is that they will put out a fine spray on quite low water pressure.

For lawn or ground cover areas an installed sprinkling system will not only cut down immeasurably on the labor involved to water those areas, but should actually improve the quality of the grass due to even watering.

The before-dinner waterer is one of the worst offenders of all. After a day of indoor confinement he enjoys to the full a brief time alone in the dusk with his trusty hose and nozzle. He waves this scepter of his office as head gardener majestically over the plants. Half an hour and the thing is done. Every leaf is moisture laden—a trap for mildew spores. The sod of the lawn is just moist enough to encourage growth of fungi, but not grass. He feels so competent, he can water his garden, front, back and sides before the evening meal can be put on the table.

This waterer is perfectly right in his method of application—he uses a sprinkling device. Then what exactly is wrong? It is all too hastily done and the timing is bad. Persons who stand and hold a hose to water become tired before enough water has fallen on the garden to do much good, and because most nozzles put out more water than the ground can absorb immediately, when water begins to run off an inexperienced gardener believes the soil wet enough for the plants' needs. Neither plants nor grass should be put to bed with wet feet.

Set sprinkler devices, on the other hand, more or less take care of themselves and are the best means of watering. They free us either for the enjoyment of the garden or for other important chores. Consider the difference between sprinkler and basin or ditch irrigation. Sprinkling collects nitrogen from the air, and if the right apparatus is used the water falls on the soil as a gentle rain. If basins or ditches are used, however, the water can be like a flood, compacting and settling the soil solidly. In most good garden soil a sprinkler gauged not to put out more water than the soil can absorb will do a thorough job on annuals and perennials in a half-hour to an hour. Longer time will be needed for trees and large shrubs. A pointed iron rod pushed into the soil will show if the moisture has penetrated deeply enough; it goes down freely, easily, only as far as the moisture has seeped.

In the rose garden and shrubbery border, as well as in a small fruit garden, flattish basins can be built to include several plants by making a low berm or ridge of soil, if water tends to run away. But if we allow this area to become flooded we defeat much of the value of using a spray, except that moisture is spread evenly over the entire area, without risk of breaking over.

A spray gives better capillarity (outward spread of water) than dribbling a hose without using any more, if as much, water. In porous soil this is important.

Mulching will conserve moisture. A mulch of straw, peat moss, leaf mold, old manure or shallow cultivation are all good in their place. But if it is difficult to cultivate at the right time it may be better to use a mulch and know the soil will be kept free from caking. Peat moss is the most elegant, and has an added advantage of being sterile. Straw lends a look of rural domesticity. Leaf mold often carries spores that are detrimental to roses and deciduous fruits. Bulk composted organic mulches are beneficial over shallow-rooted plants because cultivating them might injure their roots.

Watering methods for plants growing in containers

Location has a great deal to do with the amount of moisture a plant uses. In hot, dry, breezy situations a plant uses more moisture because of the evaporation that occurs through the leaves as well as from the soil, than it would if it were growing in a cool sheltered corner.

Think of a plant's leaves as its lungs. Moisture is evaporated through the stomata on the underside of the leaves. This keeps them crisp and outspread, but when the soil becomes too dry the leaves are limp. Feel of the leaves in midday; if they are cool and firm the plant has enough moisture.

It is impossible to set up a water schedule for a group of plants growing under varying conditions of air, temperature and light. However, there are warning signals which if heeded will help one over the first months of pot gardening. When a plant begins to wilt for lack of water, its leaves droop and the whole plant looks tired, dejected and forlorn. One wilting may do little harm, but if the condition is allowed to occur often the health of the plant will be greatly impaired.

When you are watering, don't be a miser—water thoroughly. As moisture soaks into the soil, tiny bubbles will rise through the water as the pore spaces of the soil are filled and water replaces the air in the soil.

To answer the perplexing question of when to water, one must consider the amount of evaporation that occurs through the container walls; the size of the plant in relation to the pot; the amount and kind of foliage the plant has; and, finally, the atmosphere where the plant sits.

Unglazed pots offer the greatest moisture loss of any containers, by percolation through the porous walls. Painting the pot inside with two coats of an asphalt emulsion not only retards percolation, but actually prolongs the life of the pot, and is an essential precaution when using colored paints for decorative effects.

Try this technique to lessen evaporation of unglazed pots: to maintain moisture, set one pot inside another. Allow two inches between pot sizes, which will give an inch all around, and when this space is filled with sand it will lessen evaporation.

A plant that is too large for the container will need more frequent watering than one that is in better relation to its pot size. A rule of thumb is: when a plant is twice as wide and three times as high as the pot it will soon begin to show signs of decline by blooming fiercely, by dropping much of its foliage and by lack of new growth. These are signals that the time to repot is urgent. It is wiser and more practical to develop a knowledge of a plant's needs through observation. The graceful bamboo is a good example. It may be eight times the height of the container and continue in good health, until its roots fill the soil. When repotting, prune both roots and branches to control size.

In this, as other phases of gardening, experience is the best teacher. The effect you wish to create dictates individual plant choice, and because evergreen plants tend to have more compact root systems than deciduous ones, they are better fitted to tub culture. For this reason dwarf citrus and strawberry plants are admirable. Next to the more or less permanent shrubs like holly and the mahonias come the woody perennials. English lavender and santolina are two good examples. Geraniums also excel as pot plants.

The environment—light, temperature, atmosphere and wind—affect a plant in many ways. Strong winds not only dry out soil and foliage but cause plants to give off more moisture than if they were situated in a quiet spot. Even the structure may become distorted if the wind is continuous and strong; turning a plant under those conditions will help to maintain its symmetry.

Suppose the soil has become a dry lump between watering. Thoroughly dry soil loses bulk, which creates a space between it and the container walls, and water runs away rather than soaking into the soil. You may fill this space by sifting finely pulverized soil into it, and firming it in with a thin piece of wood. If it is practicable, place the container in a tub of water to soak. For soil that is very high in peat moss this is the best way to wet it, but for planters that are too large, slow dribbling of water will eventually get it wet.

Watering potted plants can become a constant chore as summer approaches. Tin cans of various sizes and unglazed flower pots are two devices I've used to ease the task of maintaining uniform moisture. Make small nail holes in or near the bottom of the watering cans to form efficient dribblers. Holes in flower pots may be partially closed with slotted corks to provide just the amount of leak needed. Set the can or pot on the soil or rim of the tub. When filled with water a slow trickle gives thorough soaking.

Experiment with different size pots so that when filled the contents will moisten the soil of the pot or tub. They may range in size from a quart to two gallons and from six-inch to ten-inch pots. Unglazed pots blend so well with the earth that they may be left among the plants. You may want to experiment with some of the various gadgets on the market for watering pot plants, like wicks, pottery birds, etc. Almost every garden magazine issue extols the virtue of some new device.

Finally, do a thorough job of watering. If a water faucet is not convenient, save steps and perhaps even a plant with a tub or barrel from which to dip water to give first aid to pots or seed flats. Plunging small pots into basins of water is perhaps the best method to assure complete wetting. For larger containers where this method is not feasible, water slowly for a long time, employing the devices already discussed or slow dribbling. Lay a hose near the stem of the plant and let the water seep slowly until it drips freely from the drainage holes.

Spraying a fine spray of water over plants is beneficial, and has much the same effect as overhead watering in the garden. If the containers aren't too heavy and there is no danger of breaking the plants, they have an advantage in that they may be tipped over and the underside of the leaves washed for efficient insect control.

Consider irrigation not merely as giving plants a drink but a phase in complete plant nutrition; applied in connection with plant food to meet the specific needs of various plants, thrifty growth should be maintained.

Weeding techniques

Nowhere in the garden does the adage "a stitch in time saves nine" apply so aptly as it does to weeding. Like every other phase of gardening there are various methods of weeding. This chore, because it is almost always with us, looms particularly large in the work program, but sometimes by merely discussing a problem the burden is lightened. When a job is viewed from different angles, we come to know what is involved and how best to go about it, and can face up to it with courage.

Weeding is such a task. There is scarcely any time in the growing year that we are free from this onerous, time-consuming work. No matter how we approach the problem, whether with fingers, implements, chemical sprays, or even by soil fumigation, it assumes major proportions in the yearly garden routine, particularly in spring and early summer.

Weeds are seasonal, although this may be small comfort since in most areas there may be at least four kinds each season, and in favorable locations such as areas of open land receiving little weed control, they may be doubled.

Effective as chemical weed controls are, there is still hand weeding, because these poachers come up among flowers and vegetables, where a chemical can seldom be used with safety. Chemicals are expensive, and a fine degree of timing and skill is needed to warrant the cost.

Before we go into the technique of weed control by various chemical elements, let us explore some time-saving ways of getting rid of our No. 1 enemy by hand combat. One of the most serious mistakes we make in weeding is the dilatory manner in which we go about the business. A friend feels that we can enjoy the lush carpet of young weeds in the garden until they begin to usurp moisture and root space of cultivated plants, much as we enjoy kittens before they become cats.

This is not a sensible way to look at weeds, because as soon as their true leaves appear it will be easy to tell them from either flower or vegetable plants, and a scuffle hoe or long-handled spade will shave them off with little effort. As the tool is pushed ahead just beneath the soil surface, the young and tender weeds will not leave a litter to be cleaned up, but a fine-textured mulch. If left to grow large, tough fibers may become a genuine problem, not to say a lot of hard work.

I favor the push-ahead hoe for weeding, first, because it is so effortless to use and secondly, it does not leave the alternate holes and hummocks of the conventional hoe. If a long stretch-push stroke is used, somewhat after the manner of playing shuffleboard, weeding can be marvelous exercise, just strenuous enough for a cool morning. Another advantage of using this tool on hard ground is that it shaves the weeds off without the jar that would be transmitted by a conventional hoe, which should not be used on dry ground because the jar or vibration is bad for the nerves of one's shoulders and hands.

Hand weeding, that is, pulling weeds, is treacherous for hand and shoulder muscles, disfigures the fingers and is the slowest procedure; therefore, it should be done only for weeds growing among plants we are to keep. Because of the lopsided way in which we often sit when pulling weeds, the posture puts undue strain on one side and is bad for the back. By facing straight forward, however, much of the morning-after sore muscle agony so common to the beginning of the season and particularly to the arduous weekend gardener will be avoided.

Weeding on bended knees with the coordination of both hands not only gets the job done faster, but the even rhythm makes the task almost tireless. In an easy relaxed position we may nip the young weeds with our fingers much as a grazing animal feeds. Eye-to-eye contact will disclose early insect invasions that might not be seen standing. Weeds aren't just harmless little plants; many are hosts to a variety of insects and diseases that come into the garden because their favorite food plants are there. As weeds mature and toughen, insect intruders move onto more succulent plants.

Two implements to speed the labor, once the weeds directly among the plants are out of the way, are an onion weeder or a small hoe with shortened handle—either of these tools are perfect equipment for the chore and may be used with only one hand. The green carpet disappears, exposing soil for the sun to warm, to hasten maturity of flowers and vegetables.

We may slip up on a time to seed and overcome the delay by getting small plants at a nursery, but each day we neglect weeds is multiplied several times in the energy needed to get them out. No garden chore is so burdensome, none so constantly with us, but it has to be done!

It seems elementary to caution against letting weeds grow to large size, because great amounts of soil may come up with their roots, bringing desirable plants with them. After a weed has grown to this size it is beyond the pulling stage. An old butcher knife is my constant weeding companion. If one owns an asparagus cutter it is even better for cutting weeds below the crowns in the soil.

Consider weeds in areas that have not been planted, or those growing between shrubs. A spading fork offers the best conservation of both time and energy, and is very effective, because after the weeds are out the soil is almost ready to plant. Hoe manure into the top four inches to add humus and food, water well with a sprinkler and let lay for future planting. Or if a planting season is at hand, rake the beds smooth and check for adequate moisture—six inches deep is enough for annual plants.

Weatherproof knee guards are a boon for hand weeding. They require less adjusting than sponge rubber mats as you move along the ground. I use both and each serves me well—one when I am wearing a dress, the other when wearing jeans. Whichever you choose, one is an absolute must for hand weeding. I have a serviceable rough cloth bifurcated apron with commodious pockets and large padded plastic knee patches which I have found so comfortable I'm including a sketch of it for your reproduction.

Bifurcated apron of heavy duty material

Commodious pockets will hold seed packets, notepad or whatever you need to keep handy. Padded kneeling pads are always right there to prevent wet, muddy knees and encourage this comfortable posture—rather than stooping to get small plants and insects within bifocal distance!

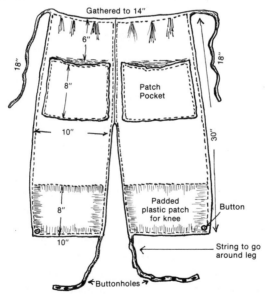

Manufacturers' packages tell in detail the advantages and limitations of chemical weed killers. However, there are unusual circumstances that should be considered in even more detail, where they are not only effective but indispensable.

Explore soil sterilization. It is obvious to most gardeners that weeds and grasses come up in places where a tool could not possibly be used to dig them out, where we do not want vegetation of any kind—between paving stones of walks or terraces, in gravel areas, driveways and similar places. Since no growth is wanted there, we may sterilize the soil. A harmless chemical is rock salt, but its action is brief. A newer method is pre-emergence, but timing is very important.

The less preferred method is spraying with oil, which not only leaves an unsightly dying weed patch or shrubs that may linger on for a while, but is offensive in other ways. Beside, it is difficult to use without staining the paving material. Sterilization and pre-emergence materials, however, prevent weeds from coming up and the solution may be dribbled into the roots of plants, leaving little if any stain. After a day or so the tops of plants may be cut off even with the ground.

Hormone sprays kill by a special action through the leaves. Be careful to use the best one for the particular plant and situation. Observe all the precautions the supplier puts on the label, and be *sure* before, not *sorry* after application.

Like other new products for gardeners, these weed killers are excellent tools when rightly used, but please don't think they are going to replace the homey task of weeding, which after all, does have its advantages—the weeds are out of the way. We can go about the routine of gardening, free from the unsightly presence of slowly dying vegetation.

There is a selective weed killer especially for dichondra. There are two very troublesome small weeds of this splendid turf—chickweed in variety and a particularly aggressive oxalis. To try to cope with these pernicious weeds by hand is not only waging a losing battle but is absolutely hopeless. Here is a problem that simply cannot be controlled by hand.

But be warned: large areas may be bare if the weed infestation is heavy and of long duration. You may think after using the chemical that it has also killed the dichondra. Mulch the bare spots with either finely screened leaf mold or peat moss to help nature stage a comeback of the dichondra turf. In a short while a thrifty dichondra lawn will appear from self-sown seeds.

Cool days are fine for clearing out overgrown brush of wild plants of blackberry, grape, ivy and poison oak. Consider these scourges one at a time. During the long days of summer with their own particular chores of watering, harvesting and plans for early planting to maintain color and yield, these unsurpers can make prodigious growth while our backs are turned.

I can almost hear the oft repeated, "But you can kill them with spray." True, but I find these woody plants easier to handle while alive, especially wild blackberry whose green thorns are less lethal than those of dead branches.

If you clear away the growth of blackberry during the summer, branch tips cannot root to form new plants, and when growth starts from live shoots in spring a minimum leaf area will need spraying, with consequently less brush to clear away. A two-year plan diligently executed should give control.

Wild grape stems of twenty or thirty feet in length climbing a choice tree often pull the tree over. Poison oak and ivy may be infectious to sensitive skin even when dormant. Clearing out by an experienced worker may be money well spent. Like wild grape, poison oak can topple trees by twining about the trunks.

Finally then, try to approach the task of weeding with planning and forethought. Use the best possible method and equipment for each kind of wild growth and situation.

Compost

What is compost? It is humusy soil made from garden waste and other materials that will hasten decay and add to the nutritive value.

Despite the fact that humus takes a large share of the garden budget, many people still begrudge the space required for composting, but if we think of compost as potpourri to be made from withering plants, it may not seem so mundane. The spicy aroma that escaped from grandmother's potpourri jars may be recaptured in next year's garden with adequate humus.

If we compare a compost pile to an iced layer cake we get an idea of the processes involved in laying it down. Garden waste represents the cake, and the soil-manure-nitrogen dressings compose the filling between the layers. When it is covered all over with a boxing of moistened soil, it does indeed resemble a massive chocolate cake.

Select a well-drained site, accessible to a garden hose for frequent sprinkling, and protected from too much sunshine. Excessive heat dries out the material and retards decomposition.

The object of making compost is two-fold: to have a ready supply of humus for potting and top-dressing garden beds, and to easily dispose of the seasonal garden trimmings, leaves and uprooted plants that otherwise could be a burden and an expense.

The value of compost depends upon what goes into it, the way it is made and how soon it is used. Refuse and soil, manure, gypsum (or lime) and an inorganic nitrogen which does not attract animals, rodents or ants but hastens decay go to make this valuable garden component. Researchers now say that the value of compost in terms of humus and nutritive value is highest before decomposition is completed, or after about six weeks, which is about the time we used to turn it. Compost laid down in autumn is ready for spring planting, and spring compost will be growth insurance for the summer and autumn garden.

Without the incantation that some people go through to make compost, the process boils down to this: piling garden wastes together into a mass with a saucer-shaped top to help retain moisture, rather than cone-shaped like a haycock.

Soil clinging to uprooted plants may be enough of that element in the compost, if placed between layers of leaves and other trimmings. The addition of agricultural gypsum and nitrogen improves the quality and nutritional content. Moisten each layer as it is made, but use only enough to wet the material, since runoff would leach out the additives. To prevent overheating, make a few three- or four-inch holes toward the center by thrusting a plant stake down through the compost pile and reaming it around, or make a tube like that shown.

Effective pens for the mellowing trash may be made from strong mesh wire—a piece ten feet long and four feet high may be formed into a circle and supported by two or three iron fence posts or 3/4-inch pipe driven into the ground. An advantage of wire over wood for the compost corral is that it may be easily removed to get at the decayed vegetation. This is about a minimum size for complete decomposition, but I've seen smaller piles made that yielded good quality humus—the trick is to use slightly more nitrogen to aid in rotting, and cover the entire mass with an airy material like burlap to lessen moisture loss.

It is better to make a small compost pile that decomposes evenly than to continue adding fresh material to a larger mass and end up with the usable humus at the inaccessible bottom. Also, compost more than a year old has little humus or plant food value; it is just good soil. Making too big a "heap" is one of the reasons gardeners become discontented with compost, which, like every other operation, has its techniques. Once understood, success is enjoyed.

Cross section of a round compost pile. Smaller composts may be made as described in the text.

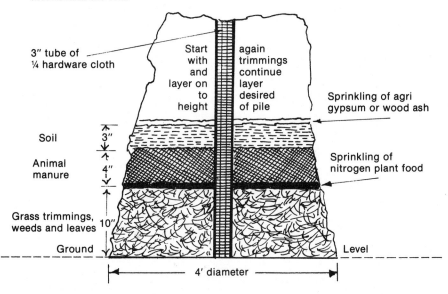

Appendixes

1. Plant food needs for a growing season

Flower, vegetable and fruit plants grouped according to their individual plant food needs for a growing season.

High	Medium	Medium low	Low
Asparagus	Broccoli	Azalea (*)	Blueberries (*)
Cabbage	Cantaloupe	Berries,	Bulbs, deciduous
Celery	Cauliflower	boysen, logan	Fruits, deciduous
Cucumber	Endive	Camellias (*)	Beans, pole and
Eggplant	Flowers, annual	Flowers,	bush
Onion	Gladiolus	perennial	Shrubs, deciduous
Pepper	Grapes	Peas, sweet	Watermelons
Potatoes	Lettuce	edible	
Spinach	Lima beans	Raspberries	
Standard (*)	Peanuts	Rhododendron (*)	*Very low*
citrus	Pumpkin	Shrubs and trees	Conifers, (*)
Avocado (*)	Squash	Broad-leafed	trees, shrubs
	Strawberry (*)	evergreens (*)	
	Sweet corn		
	Sweet potatoes		
	Vegetables, root		
	Tomato		

Note: This table will be a guide to plant-groups and the kinds to grow together.

(*) Indicates plants that need an acid soil—pH 4.5 to 6.5. Use plant foods that will produce and/or maintain that formula. A following chart will show which plant foods will do this.

The quantity of plant foods to supply the needs of plants listed above is given in the table below. The amount in pounds of dry material when applied to 100 square feet of soil areas and/or the number of applications of liquid plant food to be used either as an earth or leaf food should insure continuous growth and high yield.

217

Concentrated dry plant foods—amounts based on a formula like 5–10–5.

	lbs. per 100 ft. soil
High	4 to 5
Medium	3 to 4
Medium low	2 to 3
Low	1 to 2
Very low	½ to 1

Number of applications of liquid plant food each season of a 15–30–15 formula, based on a dilution of 1 oz. to 10 quarts of water for 40 feet foliage. Follow package directions for amounts to use on different plants, and the number of applications.

2. Analysis of some typical bulky organic mulches

Mulches	Nitrogen	Phosphoric Acid	Potash	Humus
Dairy manure	0.80	0.44	1.37	30.5
Poultry manure (floor litter)	4.17	3.15	1.56	74.0
Rabbit manure	2.05	1.35	0.83	60.0
Sheep manure	1.39	0.96	2.09	52.0
Alfalfa hay	2.46	0.60	2.09	83.6
Alfalfa straw	1.39	0.30	1.80	82.0
Lima bean straw	1.20	0.23	1.28	82.4
Grain straw	0.77	0.33	1.38	86.1
Horse manure	1.25	0.52	1.59	70.4
Tobacco litter	?	trace	4.09	70.0

Most manures have an acid pH (6.5) while hay, bean and grain straws are generally neutral (pH 7.0). Manures, in addition to sufficient nitrogen to break down (cause decay) of the fibers, contain appreciable amounts of enzymes and vitamin B_1, which other mulches lack.

Because the quality of forest humuses varies widely their analysis is not readily available. However, forest humus and oakleaf mold run from pH 6.5 to 7.0, while peatmoss and pine needle mulch are from pH 4.5 to 5.0. Vermiculite is neutral, and is valuable as an additive to potting soils and in mixes for cuttings.

3. Dressings and mulches

The following applications have been found adequate for the needs of plants.

Bulky plant foods

Light dressing—one-quarter to one-half inch finely screened manure for seed beds in open ground.

Heavy dressing and/or light mulch — one inch finely screened manure for heavy dressing or light mulch over planted areas and as a dressing for lawns.

Heavy mulch — two to four-inch dressing of manure in winter or early spring over deciduous fruits, roses. As soil conditioner for beds for flowers and vegetables.

Concentrated plant foods

Light feeding — enough complete plant food to discolor soil.

Heavy feeding—up to one-quarter inch thick—the amount used in side-dressing plants.

Side dressing — placing concentrated plant food near (beside) plants, either individual plants or along a row. This is most effective if application can be made near the end of watering, when the ground is wet enough to dissolve the nutrients into the soil.

4. Acid-alkaline reaction (pH) and nutritive values of concentrated plant foods

Acid (pH 6)	Neutral (pH 7 ±)	Alkaline (pH 8 +)	Nitrogen	Phosphoric acid	Potash
	Organic				
pH 6	Bloodmeal		8 — 12		
pH 7	Bonemeal		1 — 2	24 — 30	
pH 6	Cottonseed meal		6 — 9	2 — 6	1½ — 3
pH 6	Fish products		5 — 0	1 — 0	1 — 0
pH 8	Hardwood ash*				varies
pH 6	Urea		38 — 40		
	Chemical				
pH 6.5	Ammonium phosphate		16 — 00	20 — 00	
pH 6	Ammonium sulphate		20 — 30		
pH 6.5	Calcium sulphate (Agricultural gypsum)			97 — 00	
pH 8	Calcium carbonate (lime)			70 — 00	
pH 7	Sulphate of potash				20 — 24
pH 7	Superphosphate			18 — 00	

* Excellent light winter dressing over asparagus beds and other plants that need an alkaline soil—do not use on plants that require an acid soil.

Choose plant foods from the above groups that will nourish your plants and keep them in good health.

By having these tables grouped together in this area it will be easy to determine the kinds and amounts each column of flowers and vegetables require.

My Garden Record
Plant growth and performance

Plant name	Color	Height	Bloom	Location	Moisture	Soil

My Garden Record
Plant growth and performance

Harvest	Propagation	Pests	Control	Pruning	Summary

Index